Canadian Living's Best

30 Minutes and Light

BY

Elizabeth Baird

AND

The Food Writers of Canadian Living® Magazine
and The Canadian Living Test Kitchen

A MADISON PRESS BOOK

PRODUCED FOR

BALLANTINE BOOKS AND CANADIAN LIVING

Ballantine Books	Canadian Living
A Division of	Telemedia
Random House of	Communications Inc.
Canada Limited	25 Sheppard Avenue West
2775 Matheson Blvd East	Suite 100
Mississauga, Ontario	North York, Ontario
Canada	Canada
L4W 4P7	M2N 6S7

Canadian Cataloguing in Publication Data

Baird, Elizabeth
30 minutes and light

(Canadian living's best)
"A Madison Press book."
Includes index.
ISBN 0-345-39867-X

1. Quick and easy cookery. 2. Low-fat diet — Recipes.
I. Title. II. Title: Thirty minutes and light. IV. Series.

TX833.5.B34 1998   641.5'55   C97-932641-9

Canadian Living® is a trademark owned by
Telemedia Communications Inc. and licensed by The Madison Press Limited.
All trademark rights, registered and unregistered, are reserved worldwide.

EDITORIAL DIRECTOR: Hugh Brewster
PROJECT EDITOR: Wanda Nowakowska
EDITORIAL ASSISTANCE: Beverley Renahan, Rosemary Hillary
PRODUCTION DIRECTOR: Susan Barrable
PRODUCTION COORDINATOR: Donna Chong
BOOK DESIGN AND LAYOUT: Gordon Sibley Design Inc.
COLOR SEPARATION: Colour Technologies
PRINTING AND BINDING: Friesen Corporation

CANADIAN LIVING ADVISORY BOARD: Elizabeth Baird, Bonnie Baker Cowan,
Anna Hobbs, Caren King

CANADIAN LIVING'S BEST 30 MINUTES AND LIGHT
was produced by Madison Press Books
which is under the direction of Albert E. Cummings

Madison Press Books
40 Madison Avenue
Toronto, Ontario, Canada
M5R 2S1

Printed in Canada

Contents

Asparagus Salmon Salad (p. 22)

Cajun Rice and Beans (p. 59)

Tortilla Sandwich Melts (p. 60)

Thai Chicken Curry (p. 46)

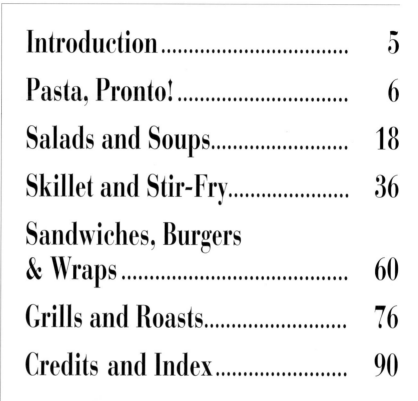

Introduction

Seeing is learning how. And that's what makes *Canadian Living's Best 30 Minutes and Light* so special. This new volume in our *Best* series includes 27 master recipes for delicious, family-pleasing main-course dishes — each with a beautiful photograph to show you how the finished supper looks plus step-by-step photos to take you through the stages from stove to table in 30 minutes or less. As a bonus, many of these how-to recipes are followed by additional recipes using the same techniques — and often the same main ingredient — so this collection of tested-till-perfect recipes is a little like getting an easy-to-follow work plan for every supper of the week.

But that's not the only reason why *30 Minutes and Light* is a cookbook we in the *Canadian Living* test kitchen and our food writers are proud to offer busy families. Because eating healthy is a top priority among Canadians, all the dishes in this timely new cookbook are as low in fat as possible — without sacrificing anything in flavor or nutrients. Most recipes also include menu suggestions and have been created around a wide variety of ingredients that are both affordable and available in supermarkets across the country.

Thirty minutes doesn't sound like much time, but it's enough to enjoy the process of cooking, to learn new healthy-cooking techniques and to come up with a delicious meal everyone will love.

Elizabeth Baird

Green Bean and Chicken Caesar Salad (p. 24)

Pasta, Pronto!

Saucy Sausage Supper ▶

For a speedy pasta supper with loads of zip, sausages save the day. Though not a low-fat food, a little sausage meat goes a long way in feeding a hungry family. And since the sausage is already seasoned, you won't need to raid the spice cabinet for this easy tomato sauce.

Per serving: about
- 465 calories
- 14 g fat
- excellent source of iron
- 24 g protein
- 62 g carbohydrate
- very high source of fiber

TIP: Serve this year-round favorite with salad and vary the greens to suit the season. In the warm months, try Boston and leaf lettuces plus spinach, watercress, radishes and cucumber. In the fall, toss together romaine, escarole and endive. During the winter, shred cabbage and mix with generous amounts of grated carrot.

12 oz	hot or sweet Italian sausages	375 g
1	can (28 oz/796 mL) tomatoes	1
1 tbsp	tomato paste	15 mL
1 tsp	fennel seeds, crushed	5 mL
3 cups	quartered mushrooms (about 8 oz/250 g)	750 mL
2	zucchini	2
4 cups	penne or rigatoni pasta	1 L
1/4 cup	freshly grated Parmesan cheese (optional)	50 mL

1 Remove casings from sausages; crumble meat into large nonstick skillet. Cook over medium-high heat, stirring occasionally, for about 5 minutes or until browned. Spoon off fat.

2 Add tomatoes, tomato paste and fennel seeds, breaking up tomatoes with back of spoon. Add mushrooms; bring to boil. Reduce heat to medium; gently boil for 10 minutes. Meanwhile, cut zucchini in half lengthwise; thinly slice crosswise. Add to pan; cook for 5 to 10 minutes or until sauce is thickened and mushrooms are tender.

3 Meanwhile, in large pot of boiling salted water, cook pasta for 8 to 10 minutes or until tender but firm. Drain well and return to pot. Add sauce; toss to coat. Serve sprinkled with Parmesan cheese (if using). Makes 4 servings.

Delicious!

Vegetable Penne

A fresh tomato sauce, chunky with zucchini and mushrooms, has its flavor smoothed with light cream cheese. Toss a salad with your favorite dressing and warm up crusty whole wheat rolls in the oven while the pasta and sauce simmer.

Per serving: about
- 610 calories
- 16 g fat
- very high source of fiber
- 19 g protein
- 99 g carbohydrate
- good source of iron

X 3	tomatoes	4
2	zucchini	2
2 tbsp	olive oil	25 mL
3	cloves garlic, minced	3
2 cups	small button mushrooms, halved	500 mL
1	onion, chopped	1
1 tbsp	dried basil	15 mL
1 tsp	each dried oregano and salt	5 mL
1/2 tsp	pepper	2 mL
Pinch	crushed hot pepper flakes	Pinch
1 tbsp	red wine vinegar	15 mL
4 oz	light cream cheese, softened	125 g
5 cups	penne	1.25 L

● Finely chop 3 of the tomatoes; cut remaining tomato into thin wedges. Quarter zucchini lengthwise; cut crosswise into slices. Set aside.

● In skillet, heat oil over medium heat; cook garlic, mushrooms, onion, basil, oregano, salt, pepper and hot pepper flakes, stirring often, for about 4 minutes or until onion is softened.

● Stir in chopped tomatoes. Increase heat to medium-high; cook, stirring occasionally, for about 5 minutes or until tomato juices are released. Stir in zucchini and vinegar. Reduce heat to medium; cook, stirring often, for about 5 minutes or until zucchini is tender. Stir in cream cheese until blended.

● Meanwhile, in large pot of boiling salted water, cook pasta for 8 to 10 minutes or until tender but firm; drain well and return to pot. Add sauce; toss to coat. Serve garnished with tomato wedges. Makes 4 servings.

TIP: Other short dry pasta such as shells, macaroni, rotini or radiatore can be substituted for penne.

PAIRING PASTA WITH SAUCES

To get the most out of a pasta dish, it's important to make a good match between pasta shapes and sauces. Within each group, the pastas can be substituted for each other in a recipe.

● **Long, thin pastas** such as spaghetti, vermicelli, spaghettini, linguine and fettuccine work well with tomato, cream, and butter and cheese sauces; strong-flavored sauces with garlic or anchovies; and fish and seafood sauces.

● Team up **short, curled or twisted pasta** shapes such as fusilli, penne and conchiglie with meat or vegetable sauces because the pasta traps tasty morsels inside and you can pick up both the pasta and chunks of meat or vegetables at the same time.

● **Small pastas** such as macaroni, stellini, orzo or tubetti are perfect for soups or stews.

● **Flat, short pastas** such as farfalle are best coated in a delicate cream, cheese or vegetable sauce.

Linguine with Clam Sauce for Two

8 oz	linguine pasta	250 g
1 tbsp	butter	15 mL
3	cloves garlic, slivered	3
1	small onion, chopped	1
1	carrot, chopped	1
1	can (5 oz/142 g) baby clams	1
2 tbsp	dry white vermouth or wine (optional)	25 mL
1/3 cup	chopped fresh parsley	75 mL
Pinch	pepper	Pinch
1/4 cup	freshly grated Parmesan cheese	50 mL

● In large pot of boiling salted water, cook pasta for 8 to 10 minutes or until tender but firm. Drain well and return to pot.

● Meanwhile, in nonstick skillet, heat butter over medium heat; cook garlic, onion and carrot, stirring occasionally, for about 4 minutes or until onion is softened. Pour in liquid from clams; add vermouth (if using). Bring to boil; boil for 3 minutes or until sauce is reduced by half and slightly thickened.

● Add clams, parsley and pepper; return to boil. Pour over pasta. Add half of the Parmesan cheese; toss to coat. Serve sprinkled with remaining Parmesan. Makes 2 servings.

Quick and easy pasta toppings can be made from cupboard staples such as canned baby clams. Enjoy with multigrain bread or rolls and a green bean salad with a mustardy dressing.

Per serving: about
- 615 calories
- 12 g fat
- good source of calcium
- excellent source of iron
- 29 g protein
- 96 g carbohydrate
- very high source of fiber

TIP: Vary the vegetables in the sauce according to what you have on hand — frozen peas, beans or broccoli are a good last-minute addition.

Veal Pizzaiola Pasta

1 lb	veal leg cutlets or pork schnitzel	500 g
1/4 tsp	each salt and pepper	1 mL
2 tsp	olive oil	10 mL
1	onion, chopped	1
2	cloves garlic, minced	2
1 tsp	dried oregano or Italian herb seasoning	5 mL
1	can (19 oz/540 mL) Italian-style stewed tomatoes	1
5 cups	rigatoni or bucatini pasta	1.25 L

● Cut veal into 1/2-inch (1 cm) wide strips; sprinkle with salt and pepper. In large nonstick skillet, heat oil over high heat; brown meat, in batches, about 2 minutes. Transfer to plate.

● Reduce heat to medium. Cook onion, garlic and oregano, stirring often, for about 5 minutes or until softened. Add tomatoes; bring to boil, breaking up with back of spoon and scraping up any brown bits. Reduce heat and simmer, stirring often, for about 8 minutes or until slightly thickened. Return meat and any accumulated juices to pan; simmer for about 2 minutes or until meat is hot.

● Meanwhile, in large pot of boiling salted water, cook pasta for 8 to 10 minutes or until tender but firm. Drain well and transfer to bowls; spoon veal mixture over top. Makes 4 servings.

Quick sauces are easier to make if your cupboard contains cans of seasoned tomatoes. Italian-style gets the nod here for a pizza-like (pizzaiola) sauce. If you don't have them, use regular stewed or plain plum tomatoes and pep them up with Italian herb seasoning. Serve with crusty rolls and a spinach salad.

Per serving: about
- 475 calories
- 6 g fat
- high source of fiber
- 36 g protein
- 67 g carbohydrate
- good source of iron

V.G. — Mike likes it

Pasta with Tomato Sauce and Greens ▲

This flavorful sauce highlights the healthful benefits of tomatoes and dark greens such as rapini or broccoli — a richness of vitamins A, C and folate, as well as naturally occurring chemicals with disease-fighting properties.

Per each of 6 servings: about
- 369 calories
- 4 g fat
- very high source of fiber
- 14 g protein
- 69 g carbohydrate
- good source of calcium and iron

1 tbsp	olive oil	15 mL
1	small onion, chopped	1
3	cloves garlic, finely chopped	3
Pinch	hot pepper flakes	Pinch
2	sweet red peppers, chopped	2
1	can (28 oz/796 mL) tomatoes	1
1 tsp	salt	5 mL
1/2 tsp	pepper	2 mL
1 lb	penne or other tubular pasta	500 g
1 lb	rapini or broccoli, trimmed and cut in 2-inch (5 cm) chunks	500 g

● In large deep skillet, heat oil over medium heat; cook onion, garlic and hot pepper flakes, stirring occasionally, for about 5 minutes or until softened. Add red peppers; cook for 5 minutes.

● Add tomatoes and juices, salt and pepper, breaking up into small pieces with fork; bring to boil. Reduce heat to medium; simmer for about 15 minutes or until thickened.

● Meanwhile, in large pot of boiling salted water, cook pasta for 6 minutes. Add rapini and return to boil; cook for 2 to 3 minutes or until rapini is tender and pasta is tender but firm. Drain well and add to sauce; toss to coat. Makes 4 to 6 servings.

TIP: If rapini is a bit too bitter for your taste, use broccoli. For a smoother sauce, purée it before tossing with pasta.

Creamy Tomato Shells

1 tbsp	vegetable oil	15 mL
2	cloves garlic, minced	2
1	onion, chopped	1
1 tbsp	dried basil	15 mL
1/2 tsp	pepper	2 mL
1/4 tsp	each salt and hot pepper sauce	1 mL
1	can (28 oz/796 mL) tomatoes	1
1 cup	2% evaporated milk	250 mL
5 cups	pasta shells	1.25 L
1/4 cup	freshly grated Parmesan cheese	50 mL

● In saucepan, heat oil over medium heat; cook garlic, onion, basil, pepper, salt and hot pepper sauce, stirring occasionally, for about 5 minutes or until softened.

● Meanwhile, in blender or food processor, purée tomatoes; add to pan and bring to boil. Reduce heat and boil gently, stirring often, for about 20 minutes or until thickened. Remove from heat; stir in milk.

● Meanwhile, in large pot of boiling salted water, cook pasta for 8 to 10 minutes or until tender but firm; drain well and return to pot. Add sauce; toss to coat. Serve sprinkled with Parmesan cheese. Makes 4 servings.

Here's a recipe with a nutritional bonus — added calcium in the form of creamy but low-fat evaporated milk. Round out the meal with a lettuce salad into which you have shredded some cabbage and carrots.

Per serving: about
- 635 calories
- 25 g protein
- 9 g fat
- 113 g carbohydrate
- excellent source of calcium and iron
- very high source of fiber

PASTA BASICS

Cook it Right
Pasta needs to be cooked in lots of water in a large pot. Here are some guidelines: For each pound (500 g) of dry pasta, use 20 cups (5 L) water and 2 tbsp (25 mL) salt. For 12 oz (375 g) of pasta, reduce the water to 16 cups (4 L) and the salt to 4 tsp (20 mL).

1 Cover and bring water and salt to full rolling boil. Add pasta, stirring to separate. Start timing the cooking from the moment the water returns to boil.

2 Boil, uncovered and stirring occasionally to prevent the pasta from sticking to the bottom of the pot, for 8 to 10 minutes for most popular shapes.

3 To see if the pasta is cooked properly, remove a piece and let it cool slightly before tasting. It is ready if it is tender but still holds its shape and is slightly firm, or *al dente*.

4 Reserve up to 1 cup (250 mL) of the cooking water in case you need to moisten your dish before serving. Pour cooked pasta into colander to drain, shaking colander slightly. Don't refresh pasta in cold water unless you are using it in a salad or in baked dishes such as lasagna.

Light Bites
● Evaporated milk adds creaminess to a sauce without all the fat.
● Instead of cheese or cream sauces, opt for tomato-, vegetable- or stock-based sauces.
● Choose low-fat sour cream, cheeses and other dairy products when possible.
● Go easy when sprinkling on the cheese at the table. Each tablespoon (15 mL) of freshly grated Parmesan adds 2 grams of fat.

Quick Nights
● Before you do anything else, put a large covered pot of water on to boil. This will take the longest time.
● For quick sauces, grate dense vegetables such as carrots and onions because they will cook faster.
● For a quick way to moisten pasta without adding extra stock, oil or sauce, save some of the pasta cooking water.

Cheesy Tortellini ▶ V.G.

*I*t's just plain clever to stock
your freezer with a selection
of instant-meal ingredients.
Frozen tortellini should be
on every busy cook's list —
just boil and toss with butter
or oil, your favorite shredded
cheese and whatever fresh
or dried herbs you have on
hand. Or try them in this
milk-smoothed ricotta sauce
tarted up with green onions
and another freezer stand-by,
frozen peas.

Per serving: about
- 560 calories
- 20 g fat
- excellent source of calcium
- 32 g protein
- 61 g carbohydrate
- good source of iron

1 lb	frozen cheese tortellini	500 g
1 cup	ricotta cheese	250 mL
3/4 cup	milk	175 mL
1 tbsp	butter	15 mL
1/4 cup	chopped green onions	50 mL
4 ~~nope~~	slices ham or prosciutto, chopped	4
Pinch	hot pepper flakes	Pinch
2/3 cup	frozen green peas	150 mL
1/2 tsp	pepper	2 mL
Pinch	nutmeg	Pinch
	Salt *fresh basil and parsley*	
1/4 cup	freshly grated Parmesan cheese	50 mL

1 In large pot of boiling salted water, cook tortellini for about 10 minutes or until tender but firm; drain well. Meanwhile, in blender or food processor, purée ricotta cheese with milk until smooth. Set aside.

2 In skillet, melt butter over medium heat; cook onions, ham and hot pepper flakes, stirring occasionally, for about 5 minutes or until onion is softened. Stir in peas.

3 Add tortellini, ricotta mixture, pepper and nutmeg; cook, stirring, for about 3 minutes or until heated through. Season with salt to taste. Serve sprinkled with Parmesan cheese. Makes 4 servings.

Fusilli with Ham and Peas ◄

1 tsp	olive oil	5 mL
1	onion, chopped	1
1	clove garlic, chopped	1
1 cup	slivered ham	250 mL
1 cup	chopped tomato	250 mL
1/2 cup	chicken stock	125 mL
1/4 cup	light cream cheese	50 mL
1 cup	frozen green peas	250 mL
1/4 tsp	each dried basil and oregano	1 mL
Pinch	pepper	Pinch
3 cups	fusilli pasta	750 mL
2 tbsp	freshly grated Parmesan cheese	25 mL

1 In large nonstick skillet, heat oil over medium heat; cook onion and garlic, stirring occasionally, for about 5 minutes or until softened. Add ham, tomato and stock; gradually blend in cream cheese, stirring until melted.

2 Add peas, basil, oregano and pepper; reduce heat and simmer for 5 minutes. Meanwhile, in large pot of boiling salted water, cook pasta for 8 to 10 minutes or until tender but firm.

3 Drain pasta well and add to skillet; toss to coat well. Serve sprinkled with Parmesan cheese. Makes 4 servings.

Ham is a wonderful treat for large gatherings, especially around holiday time. Everyone loves its smokiness and the flavor goes so well with spring, fall and winter vegetables. But with ham, especially a whole ham, comes a dilemma — what to do with leftovers? Think pasta. You don't need much ham to turn plain pasta into a feast. Serve with a beet salad made with either leftover cooked beets or drained, canned beets dressed with your favorite vinaigrette. Or try a grated carrot salad with chopped fresh parsley, lemon juice and canola oil. For an eye-catching presentation, serve either salad in a Boston lettuce cup.

Per serving: about
- 380 calories
- 19 g protein
- 9 g fat
- 54 g carbohydrate
- high source of fiber

Creamy Mushroom and Chicken Toss

Here's a lovely mellow and creamy sauce you can toss with pasta or spoon over baked or mashed potatoes or rice.

Per serving: about
- 434 calories
- 27 g protein
- 9 g fat
- 56 g carbohydrate
- high source of fiber
- excellent source of iron

2	boneless skinless chicken breasts (8 oz/250 g)	2
2 tbsp	vegetable oil	25 mL
3	onions, sliced	3
1 lb	mushrooms, sliced	500 g
1 tsp	dried thyme	5 mL
2 tbsp	all-purpose flour	25 mL
1/2 tsp	each salt and pepper	2 mL
1 cup	chicken stock	250 mL
1/2 cup	evaporated milk	125 mL
4 cups	rotini pasta	1 L
1/4 cup	chopped fresh parsley	50 mL

● Cut chicken across the grain into thin strips. In large skillet, heat half of the oil over medium-high heat; cook chicken, stirring, for about 4 minutes or until golden and no longer pink inside. Transfer to plate; keep warm.

● Add remaining oil to pan; cook onions, mushrooms and thyme, stirring occasionally, for about 10 minutes or just until mushrooms are golden and liquid is evaporated. Sprinkle with flour, salt and pepper; cook, stirring, for 1 minute. Gradually whisk in stock and evaporated milk; cook, stirring, for 2 minutes or until thickened. Stir in chicken.

● Meanwhile, in large pot of boiling salted water, cook pasta for 8 to 10 minutes or until tender but firm; drain well and return to pot. Add sauce and half of the parsley; toss to coat. Serve sprinkled with remaining parsley. Makes 4 servings.

Antipasto Toss for Two

Just like an antipasto platter to nibble on before dinner, this pasta sauce holds some cured meat, a little mellow cheese, salty olives and artichokes — the touch of exotica.

Per serving: about
- 663 calories
- 22 g protein
- 21 g fat
- 100 g carbohydrate
- very high source of fiber
- excellent source of calcium and iron

2 cups	radiatore or rotini pasta	500 mL
1-1/2 cups	pasta sauce	375 mL
1	jar (6 oz/170 mL) marinated artichoke hearts, drained and chopped	1
1/3 cup	sliced black olives	75 mL
2 oz	capocollo or salami, chopped (optional)	60 g
1/2 cup	cubed mozzarella cheese	125 mL

● In large pot of boiling salted water, cook pasta for 8 to 10 minutes or until tender but firm; drain well and return to pot.

● Meanwhile, in saucepan, heat pasta sauce over medium-low heat until bubbling. Stir in artichokes, olives, and capocollo (if using); stir into pasta. Gently stir in half of the mozzarella cheese until melted. Serve sprinkled with remaining mozzarella. Makes 2 servings.

PARMESAN CHEESE

Buy Parmesan cheese in a chunk and grate it as needed in the kitchen or at the table, as they do in Parma, Italy, where the cheese is made. The name for authentic Parmesan cheese is Parmigiano Reggiano and the real cheese always carries that name stamped on its rind. While it's true that Parmigiano Reggiano is expensive, it's a well-made, well-aged cheese and a little goes a long way. Of course, you can use any of your favorite sharp cheeses if Parmigiano Reggiano is not available — Romano or Asiago are good Italian replacements, as are old Cheddar or Gruyère. Avoid imitation Parmesans as they tend to be strong with no underlying mellowness.

V G – 50-50

Spinach Pesto and Ricotta ▲

5 cups	fusilli pasta	1.25 L
2 tbsp	butter	25 mL
1	onion, chopped	1
3	cloves garlic, minced	3
1	pkg (10 oz/300 g) fresh spinach, trimmed	1
1 tbsp	dried basil	15 mL
1 tsp	salt	5 mL
1/2 tsp	pepper	2 mL
1 cup	ricotta cheese	250 mL
1/3 cup	freshly grated Parmesan cheese	75 mL
2 tbsp	lemon juice	25 mL
2 tbsp	pine nuts, toasted	25 mL

● In large pot of boiling salted water, cook pasta for 8 to 10 minutes or until tender but firm. Reserving 1/2 cup (125 mL) cooking water, drain pasta and return to pot.

● Meanwhile, in large skillet or Dutch oven, melt 1 tbsp (15 mL) of the butter over medium heat; cook onion and garlic, stirring occasionally, for 5 minutes or until softened. Stir in spinach and basil; cover and cook for 2 minutes. Uncover and cook, stirring, for 2 minutes longer. Transfer to food processor. Add remaining butter, salt and pepper; purée until smooth. Add reserved pasta water; blend well.

● Add spinach mixture to pasta along with 3/4 cup (175 mL) of the ricotta cheese, Parmesan cheese and lemon juice; toss to combine. Serve each with dollop of remaining ricotta; sprinkle with pine nuts. Makes 4 servings.

When the frost has nipped your fresh basil or it's covered with snow, let spinach and dry basil rekindle its delicious flavors in a toss of fusilli.

Per serving: about
● 637 calories
● 21 g fat
● very high source of fiber
● 27 g protein
● 86 g carbohydrate
● excellent source of calcium and iron

Salads and Soups

Deli Rice Salad Supper ▶

Fluffy rice — the grains beautifully separate and liberally freckled with the reds and greens of tomatoes, fresh basil and green peppers — turns into a satisfying main course when deli smoked turkey and ham are added to the mix. Options for the turkey and ham abound, including cold leftover roast or barbecued chicken, turkey or fish. Pantry possibilities include canned water-packed tuna or sockeye salmon, or drained canned kidney beans, chick-peas or lentils. While the rice cooks, there is plenty of time to chop vegetables and herbs and to wash greens. Round out the menu with whole grain rolls or bread.

Per serving: about
- 295 calories
- 12 g fat
- good source of iron
- 13 g protein
- 36 g carbohydrate

3/4 cup	long-grain rice	175 mL
6 oz	sliced smoked turkey or ham	175 g
4	green onions, chopped	4
2	tomatoes, diced	2
1	sweet green pepper, chopped	1
1/4 cup	chopped fresh basil	50 mL
1/2 tsp	each salt and pepper	2 mL
	Lettuce leaves	
8	black olives, sliced	8
	DRESSING	
3 tbsp	cider vinegar	50 mL
2 tbsp	olive oil	25 mL
1	clove garlic, minced	1

1 In saucepan, bring 1-1/2 cups (375 mL) water to boil; add rice and reduce heat to low. Cover and cook for 20 minutes or until rice is tender; let cool. Fluff with fork.

2 Slice turkey into 1/2-inch (1 cm) wide strips. In large bowl, gently toss together rice, turkey, onions, tomatoes, green pepper, basil, salt and pepper.

3 DRESSING: Whisk together vinegar, oil and garlic; pour over rice mixture and toss gently. Spoon into lettuce-lined bowls; garnish with olives. Makes 4 servings.

Bulgur Tuna Tabbouleh

Tuna adds a new twist to a classic tabbouleh. Spoon tabbouleh into lettuce cups (Boston is ideal) and toast pita breads to go alongside.

Per serving: about
- 335 calories
- 25 g protein
- 13 g fat
- 30 g carbohydrate
- very high source of fiber
- good source of iron

1 cup	bulgur	250 mL
2	cans (6.5 oz/184 g each) white tuna, drained	2
3/4 cup	chopped fresh flat leaf parsley	175 mL
1	large tomato, chopped	1
	DRESSING	
3 tbsp	white wine vinegar	50 mL
2 tbsp	extra virgin olive oil	25 mL
1/2 tsp	salt	2 mL
1/4 tsp	pepper	1 mL

● In large bowl, pour 3 cups (750 mL) boiling water over bulgur; let stand for 10 minutes. Drain well and return to bowl; let cool. Add tuna, parsley and tomato; toss gently.

● DRESSING: In small bowl, whisk together vinegar, oil, salt and pepper; pour over tabbouleh and toss to coat. *(Tabbouleh can be covered and refrigerated for up to 4 hours.)* Makes 4 servings.

TIPS

● Because bulgur has already been cooked, it just needs to be rehydrated, and it's this short preparation time that makes bulgur so appealing for quick main-course salads and side dishes. Its nutty taste is also a perfect match for the fresh parsley and tomato of a traditional Lebanese salad as well as for other fresh ingredients.

● Because the acid level in vinegars can vary, you may want to add up to 1 tbsp (15 mL) more white wine vinegar if you prefer more tang.

Potato Salad with Shrimp

Potatoes with the skins on are a good source of complex carbohydrates and fiber. You can substitute salmon for the shrimp, if you like. Enjoy with crusty brown rolls or pumpernickel bread and corn on the cob or sliced tomatoes.

Per serving: about
- 250 calories
- 19 g protein
- 9 g fat
- 23 g carbohydrate
- good source of iron

1 lb	small red potatoes (about 6), unpeeled	500 g
1/2 cup	chopped celery	125 mL
1/4 cup	chopped red onion	50 mL
2 tbsp	chopped fresh parsley	25 mL
1	hard-cooked egg	1
6 oz	cooked shrimp	175 g
	DRESSING	
1/4 cup	ricotta cheese	50 mL
2 tbsp	freshly grated Parmesan cheese	25 mL
1/4 cup	milk	50 mL
1 tbsp	olive oil	15 mL
1 tbsp	white wine vinegar	15 mL
1 tsp	Dijon mustard	5 mL
1/4 tsp	salt	1 mL
Pinch	pepper	Pinch
1	clove garlic, minced	1

● Scrub potatoes. In saucepan of boiling salted water, cover and cook potatoes for 20 minutes or just until tender. Drain and cut into bite-size chunks.

● DRESSING: Meanwhile, in blender, blend together ricotta and Parmesan cheeses, milk, oil, vinegar, mustard, salt and pepper until smooth. Stir in garlic.

● In bowl, combine potatoes, celery, onion and parsley; add dressing and toss to coat. *(Salad can be prepared to this point, covered and refrigerated for up to 1 day.)* Slice egg; arrange egg and shrimp over salad. Makes 4 servings.

Mexican-Style Bean Salad

1	can (19 oz/540 mL) black or kidney beans	1
1	can (19 oz/540 mL) romano beans	1
1 cup	cooked corn kernels	250 mL
1/2 cup	thinly sliced onion	125 mL
Half	sweet red pepper, chopped	Half
4	black olives, sliced	4
2 tbsp	chopped fresh coriander or parsley	25 mL
	DRESSING	
1/3 cup	lemon juice	75 mL
2 tbsp	vegetable oil	25 mL
2 tsp	granulated sugar	10 mL
1/4 tsp	salt	1 mL
Pinch	pepper	Pinch

● Drain and rinse black and romano beans; drain again and place in bowl. Add corn, onion, red pepper and olives.

● DRESSING: In small bowl, whisk together lemon juice, oil, sugar, salt and pepper; pour over bean mixture. Sprinkle with coriander; toss to coat. Makes 6 servings.

With two different kinds of beans plus corn, this is a colorful salad. But it needs crusty rolls and a plate of sliced tomatoes and cucumbers to round out the menu.

Per serving: about
- 250 calories
- 6 g fat
- very high source of fiber
- 12 g protein
- 39 g carbohydrate

[handwritten: or 1 cup quinoa boiled in 2 cups water or chicken/vegetable broth]

Greek Pasta Salad V.G

1 cup	fusilli pasta	250 mL
Quarter	seedless cucumber	Quarter
Half	sweet green pepper, coarsely chopped	Half
6	cherry tomatoes, halved	6
2	green onions, chopped	2
1/2 cup	cooked or canned chick-peas	125 mL
1/2 cup	artichoke hearts, cut in bite-size pieces	125 mL
1/4 cup	black olives, quartered	50 mL
1 oz	feta cheese, crumbled	25 g
	Salt and pepper	
	DRESSING	
1 tbsp	olive oil	15 mL
1 tbsp	red wine vinegar	15 mL
2 tsp	lemon juice	10 mL
1	clove garlic, minced	1
1/2 tsp	dried oregano	2 mL

[handwritten: or apple cider vinegar]

● In large pot of boiling salted water, cook pasta for 8 to 10 minutes or until tender but firm; drain and rinse under cold water. Drain again and place in bowl.

● Cut cucumber into 3/4-inch (2 cm) chunks. Add to pasta along with green pepper, tomatoes, onions, chick-peas, artichoke hearts, olives and feta cheese.

● DRESSING: In small bowl, whisk together 1 tbsp (15 mL) water, oil, vinegar, lemon juice, garlic and oregano. Pour over salad; toss to coat. Season with salt and pepper to taste. *(Salad can be covered and refrigerated for up to 2 days.)* Makes 3 servings.

Sunny Greek salad ingredients — tomatoes and cucumbers cut on the chunky side, olives and feta cheese plus pasta and chick-peas — fire up energy any time of the year. Serve with crusty bread for dinner or for a power-packed lunch.

Per serving: about
- 260 calories
- 9 g fat
- high source of fiber
- 9 g protein
- 37 g carbohydrate
- good source of iron

Asparagus Salmon Salad ◀

1 lb	asparagus	500 g
10 cups	torn salad greens	2.5 L
1 cup	sliced mushrooms	250 mL
3	green onions, sliced	3
4	salmon fillets (1 lb/500 g)	4
	DRESSING	
1/4 cup	light mayonnaise	50 mL
2 tsp	Dijon mustard	10 mL
1/4 tsp	each grated lemon rind, salt and pepper	1 mL
Pinch	granulated sugar	Pinch
1	clove garlic, minced	1
2/3 cup	buttermilk	150 mL
1 tbsp	chopped fresh dill	15 mL
1 tbsp	lemon juice	15 mL

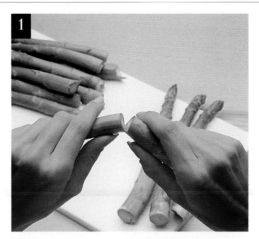

1 Snap tough (woody) ends off asparagus; cut stalks diagonally into 2-inch (5 cm) lengths. In saucepan of boiling salted water, cook asparagus for 3 minutes or until tender-crisp; drain and cool in cold water. Pat dry and place in bowl. Add salad greens, mushrooms and onions.

2 DRESSING: In small bowl, whisk together mayonnaise, mustard, lemon rind, salt, pepper, sugar and garlic. Remove 1 tbsp (15 mL); brush over top and sides of fish. Broil, skin side down, on greased rack for 5 to 7 minutes or just until fish flakes easily when tested with fork.

3 Meanwhile, whisk buttermilk, dill and lemon juice into remaining dressing; pour over greens and toss to coat. Arrange greens on plates. Peel skin off each fillet; place on salad. Makes 4 servings.

In cold weather, hearty ingredients satisfy our appetites best. But when the spring sun streams in our windows and the stores are filled with fresh local asparagus and vibrant green leaf lettuces, we welcome the lightness of dinner-size salads. This one has a ranch-style buttermilk dressing that coats the greens nicely and complements the richness of the starring ingredient — broiled or grilled salmon.

Per serving: about
- 265 calories
- 27 g protein
- 12 g fat
- 13 g carbohydrate
- high source of fiber
- excellent source of iron

TIP: When choosing salmon, note that a 4-oz (125 g) fillet portion may seem small but is in fact quite satisfying and will look more generous if you choose broader pieces near the tail.

Green Bean and Chicken Caesar Salad ▶

Italian chef Caesar Cardini may have tossed his first Caesar salad more than 70 years ago in Tijuana, Mexico, but this bold, refreshing classic has lost none of its appeal. Here, it's crunchy green beans that team up with the time-honored (but lower-fat) dressing to guarantee a delightful main course. Add grilled or oven-warmed focaccia bread to the menu.

Per serving: about
• 284 calories
• 13 g fat
• 30 g protein
• 12 g carbohydrate

3	boneless skinless chicken breasts (1 lb/500 g)	3
Pinch	each salt and pepper	Pinch
1 lb	green beans	500 g
1	sweet red pepper	1
8	large lettuce leaves	8
	DRESSING	
3 tbsp	extra virgin olive oil	50 mL
2 tbsp	freshly grated Parmesan cheese	25 mL
2 tbsp	chicken stock	25 mL
2 tbsp	white wine vinegar	25 mL
3	cloves garlic, minced	3
2 tsp	Dijon mustard	10 mL
1-1/2 tsp	anchovy paste	7 mL
1/4 tsp	pepper	1 mL
1/4 tsp	Worcestershire sauce	1 mL

1 DRESSING: In small bowl, whisk together oil, Parmesan cheese, stock, vinegar, garlic, mustard, anchovy paste, pepper and Worcestershire sauce; remove 2 tbsp (25 mL) and set aside. Season chicken with salt and pepper. Place on greased grill over medium heat; close lid and cook, turning once and basting with reserved 2 tbsp (25 mL) dressing, for 10 minutes or until no longer pink inside. Transfer to cutting board; tent with foil and let stand for 5 minutes.

2 Meanwhile, trim beans; cut diagonally into 2-inch (5 cm) lengths. In saucepan of lightly salted boiling water, cook beans for 5 minutes or until tender-crisp. Drain and cool under cold water; drain again and pat dry.

3 Cut red pepper in half crosswise; seed, core and cut lengthwise into thin strips. Slice chicken across the grain into thin strips. In large bowl, combine beans, red pepper and chicken; add dressing and toss to coat. Serve on lettuce-lined plates. Makes 4 servings.

Stir-Fry Pork Tenderloin Salad

1	pkg (10 oz/284 g) fresh spinach	1
Half	each sweet red and yellow pepper	Half
12 oz	pork tenderloin	375 g
1 lb	asparagus	500 g
1 tbsp	vegetable oil	15 mL
1	clove garlic, minced	1
	MUSTARD HONEY DRESSING	
2 tbsp	rice wine vinegar	25 mL
1 tbsp	vegetable oil	15 mL
1 tbsp	each liquid honey and soy sauce	15 mL
2 tsp	Dijon mustard	10 mL
1/4 tsp	pepper	1 mL

● Tear spinach into bite-size pieces; place in large bowl. Cut red and yellow peppers into strips; add to bowl. Slice pork into 1/4-inch (5 mm) thick rounds; cut in half and set aside.

● Snap tough (or woody) ends off asparagus; cut stalks into 2-inch (5 cm) lengths. In skillet, bring 1/2 inch (1 cm) water to boil; simmer asparagus for 3 minutes or until tender-crisp. Drain and cool under cold water; drain, pat dry and add to bowl.

● MUSTARD HONEY DRESSING: In small bowl, whisk together vinegar, oil, honey, soy sauce, mustard and pepper; set aside.

● In skillet, heat oil over high heat; stir-fry pork and garlic for 3 minutes or just until pork is no longer pink. Add dressing and toss to coat. Add to bowl; toss well. Makes 4 servings.

Pork tenderloin is meltingly tender and lean — a perfect ingredient for a healthful warm salad. Start the meal with a glass of chilled tomato juice and accompany the salad with grainy rolls.

Per serving: about
- 230 calories
- 23 g protein
- 10 g fat
- 14 g carbohydrate
- high source of fiber
- excellent source of iron

Grilled Chicken Pasta Salad ▶

Here's a delicious summer plateful of pasta, grilled chicken and garden-fresh peppers, tomatoes and basil. Toast a flatbread or pita alongside the chicken on the grill and when corn's in season, cook cobs in the microwave to have before the salad, or after.

Per serving: about
- 585 calories
- 14 g fat
- very high source of fiber
- 34 g protein
- 80 g carbohydrate
- good source of iron

TIP: Time management in the kitchen translates into grilling enough chicken one evening so you have enough hot for one meal, with leftovers for the next day's dinner salad. Try this trick when you want chicken for sandwiches or traditional chicken salads, too.

3	boneless skinless chicken breasts (1 lb/500 g)	3
3 tbsp	vegetable oil	50 mL
3 tbsp	red wine vinegar	50 mL
1 tbsp	Dijon mustard	15 mL
2	green onions, chopped	2
2	cloves garlic, minced	2
1/2 tsp	salt	2 mL
1/4 tsp	each pepper and granulated sugar	1 mL
4 cups	fusilli pasta	1 L
1	each sweet yellow and green pepper, chopped	1
2	tomatoes, seeded and chopped	2
1/3 cup	chopped fresh basil	75 mL

1 Place chicken in shallow dish. In small bowl, whisk together oil, vinegar, 1 tbsp (15 mL) water, mustard, onions, garlic, salt, pepper and sugar; remove 2 tbsp (25 mL) and brush over chicken. Let stand for 10 minutes.

2 Place chicken on greased grill over medium-high heat; close lid and cook, turning once, for 8 to 10 minutes or until chicken is no longer pink inside. Slice diagonally into thin strips.

3 In large pot of boiling salted water, cook pasta for 8 to 10 minutes or until tender but firm. Drain and cool under cold water; drain well. In bowl, combine pasta, chicken, yellow and green peppers, tomatoes and basil; toss with remaining dressing. Makes 4 servings.

White Bean Soup with Carrot Salsa ◄

1 tsp	vegetable oil	5 mL
1	onion, chopped	1
2	cloves garlic, minced	2
3/4 tsp	each ground cumin and coriander	4 mL
2	cans (19 oz/540 mL each) white kidney beans, drained and rinsed	2
3 cups	vegetable or chicken stock	750 mL
	Salt and pepper	
	CARROT SALSA	
1	carrot, grated	1
4 tsp	chopped fresh coriander or parsley	20 mL
1 tsp	lemon juice	5 mL
1/2 tsp	vegetable oil	2 mL

1 In saucepan, heat oil over medium heat; cook onion and garlic, stirring occasionally, for 3 minutes or until softened. Add cumin and ground coriander; cook for 1 minute. Add beans and stock; bring to boil. Reduce heat, cover and simmer for 15 minutes.

2 CARROT SALSA: Meanwhile, in bowl, stir together carrot, fresh coriander, lemon juice and oil; set aside.

3 In food processor or blender, purée soup until smooth; if necessary, return to saucepan and heat through. Season with salt and pepper to taste. Ladle into bowls; top with carrot salsa. Makes 4 servings.

*H*omemade soup in 30 minutes is a delicious reality, thanks to this very light, fiber- and iron-rich soup. Canned beans plus chicken or vegetable stock are the convenience products that make it possible. But what lifts a simple soup into the special-tasting sphere is the zesty toss of grated carrot on top. Try it with chopped coriander for a salsa flavor, or use a favorite fresh herb such as basil, dill, parsley or chives. Serve with pita crisps or oven-warmed tortillas. Afterward, enjoy a green salad.

Per serving: about
- 275 calories
- 17 g protein
- 4 g fat
- 47 g carbohydrate
- very high source of fiber
- good source of iron

TIP: Coriander is a fresh green herb also known as cilantro or Chinese parsley. It is the most widely used herb in the world.

OK

Clean-Out-the-Crisper Creamy Soup

This soup is comfort without the calories — we call it creamy because that's how it tastes and looks. The creaminess comes from milk plus puréeing part of the soup to create a smooth backdrop for the rest of the chunky vegetables.

Per serving: about
• 165 calories
• 4 g fat
• high source of fiber
• 10 g protein
• 24 g carbohydrate

1 tsp	vegetable oil	5 mL
1	onion, chopped	1
2	carrots, chopped	2
2	cloves garlic, minced	2
1/2 tsp	each dried thyme and oregano	2 mL
3 cups	chicken or vegetable stock	750 mL
1	potato, peeled and chopped	1
2 cups	chopped broccoli	500 mL
1 cup	frozen peas	250 mL
1 cup	milk	250 mL
1/2 tsp	salt	2 mL
Pinch	pepper	Pinch

● In large saucepan, heat oil over medium heat; cook onion, carrots, garlic, thyme and oregano, stirring occasionally, for 5 minutes or until onion is softened.

● Add stock, potato and broccoli; bring to boil. Reduce heat, cover and simmer for 15 minutes or until potato is very tender. Add peas; cook for 5 minutes.

● Pour half into blender; purée until smooth. Return to saucepan. Stir in milk, salt and pepper; heat until steaming. Makes 4 servings.

Turkey Hot Pot — Olé   *V.G. - thick!*

Post-holiday kitchens almost always include leftover turkey, and sometimes even turkey stock. Instead of simmering up an ordinary turkey soup, give these ingredients a fling with Mexican flavors and top with a thatch of shredded Cheddar or Monterey Jack cheese.

Per each of 8 servings: about
• 289 calories
• 6 g fat
• good source of iron
• 21 g protein
• 38 g carbohydrate
• very high source of fiber

2 tbsp	vegetable oil	25 mL
1	large onion, coarsely chopped	1
1	large clove garlic, minced	1
1/2 tsp	hot pepper flakes	2 mL
3	potatoes, peeled and cubed	3
4 cups	turkey or chicken stock	1 L
1 tsp	dried oregano	5 mL
1	can (19 oz/540 mL) tomatoes	1
1	can (14 oz/398 mL) pinto or kidney beans, drained and rinsed	1
2 cups	frozen lima beans	500 mL
2 cups	diced cooked turkey	500 mL
1-1/2 cups	corn kernels	375 mL
3 tbsp	chopped fresh coriander or parsley	50 mL
1 tbsp	lime or lemon juice	15 mL
	Salt and pepper	

● In large saucepan, heat oil over medium heat; cook onion, garlic and hot pepper flakes, stirring, for 3 to 5 minutes or until softened.

● Add potatoes, stock and oregano; cover and simmer for 10 to 15 minutes or until potatoes are tender.

● Add tomatoes, breaking up with spoon; add pinto and lima beans, turkey and corn. Simmer, covered, for 5 minutes or until lima beans are tender. Stir in coriander, lime juice, and salt and pepper to taste. Makes 6 to 8 servings.

Heartwarming Hamburger Soup ▲

8 oz	lean ground beef	250 g
1	each onion and carrot, chopped	1
1	stalk celery, chopped	1
2	cloves garlic, minced	2
1-1/2 tsp	dried basil or marjoram	7 mL
1/4 tsp	each salt and pepper	1 mL
1	can (19 oz/540 mL) tomatoes	1
1	can (10 oz/284 mL) beef stock	1
1-1/2 cups	water	375 mL
1-1/2 tsp	Worcestershire sauce	7 mL
2 cups	cubed peeled potatoes	500 mL
1 cup	cubed zucchini	250 mL
1/2 cup	small shell pasta	125 mL

● In large saucepan, cook beef over medium-high heat, breaking up with spoon, for 3 to 5 minutes or until no longer pink; drain off any fat. Add onion, carrot, celery, garlic, basil, salt and pepper; cook, stirring often, for about 5 minutes or until onion is softened.

● Add tomatoes, breaking up with spoon. Stir in stock, water and Worcestershire sauce; bring to boil. Stir in potatoes. Reduce heat, cover and simmer for 10 minutes.

● Stir in zucchini and pasta; cook, covered, for 8 to 10 minutes or until pasta is tender but firm. Makes 4 servings.

Ground beef is great for a quick soup because it doesn't need to cook for hours to tenderize.

Per serving: about
- 261 calories
- 6 g fat
- good source of iron
- 17 g protein
- 35 g carbohydrate
- high source of fiber

TIP: Authentic Worcestershire sauce is a handy flavoring ingredient to keep in your quick-and-healthy cooking cupboard. Made from a variety of ingredients and aged for years, the sauce will add depth and mellowness to soups, stews and marinades, to name just a few of its many uses.

Minestrone in Minutes ◀

2	carrots	2
1	large potato, peeled	1
1	onion	1
1	stalk celery	1
2 tbsp	olive oil	25 mL
1	clove garlic, minced	1
1/4 tsp	dried rosemary	1 mL
1/2 cup	broken spaghetti	125 mL
2	cans (10 oz/284 mL each) chicken stock	2
5 cups	packed fresh spinach (half 10 oz/284 g pkg)	1.25 L
	Freshly grated Parmesan cheese	

1 Cut carrots, potato, onion and celery into bite-size chunks. In large saucepan, heat oil over medium heat; cook vegetables, garlic and rosemary, covered and stirring occasionally, for 5 minutes.

2 Stir in pasta, then stock and 2 stock cans of water; bring to boil. Boil gently for about 15 minutes or until pasta and vegetables are tender.

3 Stack spinach leaves; slice into thin strips. Stir into soup; heat for about 1 minute or just until wilted. Serve immediately, sprinkled with Parmesan cheese. Makes 4 servings.

TIP: High sodium counts are the worry when using canned broths and stocks, as well as stock made from cubes or powders. Look for the product with the lowest sodium or salt content.

*F*orget the notion that old-fashioned long simmering is required for a great-tasting minestrone. Chunky vegetables, pasta in the form of broken spaghetti and a final flourish of fresh spinach make this minestrone quick, satisfying and as close to the Italian original as you can get in under 30 minutes. While the minestrone simmers, brush a mixture of olive oil, minced garlic and dried oregano over thickly sliced Italian or French bread and toast in the oven until crisp and golden.

Per serving: about
- 250 calories
- 11 g protein
- 9 g fat
- 31 g carbohydrate
- good source of iron

Chinese-Style Quickie Noodle Soup ▶

Chinese egg drop soup and Italian stracciatella, the starting formulas for our soups, are both simple, comforting broths with seasonings and eggs stirred in at the end. Vegetables and noodles provide substance and main-course appeal.

Per serving: about
- 149 calories
- 4 g fat
- high source of fiber
- 9 g protein
- 21 g carbohydrate

1	can (10 oz/284 mL) chicken stock	1
2 cups	mixed frozen vegetables	500 mL
1 cup	fine egg noodles	250 mL
1 tbsp	cornstarch	15 mL
1	egg, lightly beaten	1
1 tbsp	sodium-reduced soy sauce	15 mL
1 tsp	sesame oil	5 mL
1	green onion, sliced	1

● In large saucepan, bring stock and 3 cups (750 mL) water to boil. Add vegetables; cover and return to boil. Add noodles; cook, uncovered and stirring occasionally, for 5 minutes.

● Meanwhile, dissolve cornstarch in 1 tbsp (15 mL) cold water. Add to boiling stock mixture; cook, stirring, for about 1 minute or until clear. Slowly pour in egg and stir once. Turn off heat. Stir in soy sauce and oil. Serve garnished with onion. Makes 4 servings.

VARIATION

● ITALIAN-STYLE QUICKIE NOODLE SOUP: In saucepan, bring 1 can (10 oz/284 mL) chicken stock and 3 cups (750 mL) water to boil. Add 2 cups (500 mL) mixed frozen vegetables; cover and return to boil. Add 1 cup (250 mL) fine egg noodles; cook, uncovered and stirring, for 5 minutes. In bowl, lightly beat 2 eggs; stir in 2 tbsp (25 mL) freshly grated Parmesan cheese, 1 tbsp (15 mL) chopped fresh parsley and pinch each grated nutmeg and pepper. Stir into pan. Reduce heat and simmer, stirring, for 2 minutes. Makes 4 servings.

TIP: You can substitute 1-1/4 cups (300 mL) vegetable stock for the can of chicken stock.

Kid-Pleasing Chicken Soup

Even without the chicken, this main-course soup is a must-make. Kids love the star or alphabet pasta shapes — maybe they can find their name in the broth! Serve with tortilla chips made from crisping and browning fresh or stale tortillas in the oven.

Per serving: about
- 280 calories
- 4 g fat
- good source of iron
- 27 g protein
- 33 g carbohydrate

3	boneless skinless chicken breasts (1 lb/500 g)	3
2 tsp	vegetable oil	10 mL
2	cloves garlic, minced	2
1	onion, chopped	1
1/2 tsp	each chili powder and dried oregano	2 mL
1	each sweet red and green pepper, chopped	1
1	can (19 oz/540 mL) tomatoes, drained and chopped	1
5 cups	chicken stock	1.25 L
1 cup	stellini or alphabet pasta	250 mL
3/4 cup	cooked corn kernels	175 mL
	Lime or lemon wedges	

● Cut chicken across the grain into 1/4-inch (5 mm) thick strips; set aside.

● In large saucepan or Dutch oven, heat oil over medium heat; cook garlic, onion, chili powder and oregano, stirring occasionally, for 5 minutes or until softened.

● Add chicken and red and green peppers; cook for 5 minutes or just until chicken is no longer pink inside. Add tomatoes and stock; bring to boil.

● Add pasta; simmer over medium heat, stirring occasionally, for 6 minutes or until pasta is tender but firm. Stir in corn. Serve with lime wedges. Makes 6 servings.

Skillet and Stir-Fry

Sautéed Hoisin Orange Chicken ▶

Sunny citrus flavors deliciously define this fresh and fast supper — a perfect meal to salute the lighter days of summer. And the meal is light, too. By just removing the skin from the chicken, you eliminate about 5 grams of fat per serving. Sauté the chicken, then simmer the orangy sauce to pour over top. While the chicken cooks, minimize clutter and cleanup by steaming some asparagus on top of the boiling water for the noodles.

Per serving: about
- 212 calories
- 6 g fat
- 29 g protein
- 10 g carbohydrate

4	boneless skinless chicken breasts (1lb/500 g)	4
Pinch	each salt and pepper	Pinch
1 tbsp	vegetable oil	15 mL
1	clove garlic, minced	1
1 tsp	grated orange rind	5 mL
1/2 cup	orange juice	125 mL
1/4 cup	hoisin sauce	50 mL
Pinch	hot pepper flakes	Pinch
	Carrot cutouts, chive sprigs and long Italian radicchio (optional)	

1 Sprinkle chicken with salt and pepper. In nonstick skillet, heat oil over medium-high heat; cook chicken, turning once, for 8 to 10 minutes or until golden and no longer pink inside. Transfer to plate; keep warm.

2 Add garlic to skillet; cook for 1 minute. Combine orange rind and juice, hoisin sauce and hot pepper flakes. Add to skillet and bring to boil; cook, stirring, for 3 minutes or until thickened slightly.

3 Return chicken to skillet, turning to coat; heat through. To serve, slice chicken and spoon sauce over top. Garnish with carrot cutouts, chive sprigs and long Italian radicchio (if using). Makes 4 servings.

Pork Chop Skillet Supper ◀

4	pork loin chops (1-1/2 lb/750 g)	4
2	cloves garlic, minced	2
2 tsp	crumbled dried rosemary	10 mL
2 tsp	olive oil	10 mL
1	red or yellow onion, sliced	1
1 cup	parboiled rice	250 mL
1	each sweet red and green pepper, chopped	1
Pinch	salt	Pinch
1-1/2 cups	chicken stock	375 mL
1/4 cup	Kalamata olives, quartered	50 mL

1 Trim any fat from chops; sprinkle both sides with garlic and half of the rosemary. In skillet, heat oil over medium heat; cook chops, turning once, for about 8 minutes or until juices run clear when chops are pierced and just a hint of pink remains inside. Transfer to plate.

2 Add onion to pan; cook, stirring often, for 3 minutes or until softened. Add rice, stirring to coat. Add red and green peppers, salt and remaining rosemary.

3 Pour in stock and bring to boil; reduce heat, cover and simmer for 20 minutes or until rice is tender. Arrange chops on top; cover and cook until heated through, about 5 minutes. Sprinkle with olives. Makes 4 servings.

Suppers that please the whole family come from creative cooks like Kate Gammal, a trained chef and mother of two energetic boys. Keeping all the cooking in one pot — in this case, a skillet — means less tending and less clean-up. And that's a family pleaser for sure. While the pork chops and rice simmer in Mediterranean flavors, toss cucumbers in a yogurt-herb dressing to serve alongside.

Per serving: about
- 390 calories
- 24 g protein
- 12 g fat
- 45 g carbohydrate

Plum-Glazed Pork Chops

Take-out and pick-up meals are handy and as close as your phone or store, but they're also an expensive way to solve the rush-hour dinner dilemma. Instead, stock items such as plum sauce to add to fridge staples. You'll be able to serve a homemade dish your family will love at a fraction of the cost.

Per serving: about
- 265 calories
- 9 g fat
- 22 g protein
- 21 g carbohydrate

4	boneless pork chops (1 lb/500 g)	4
1/4 tsp	each salt and pepper	1 mL
1 tbsp	vegetable oil	15 mL
1	sweet red or green pepper, chopped	1
1	onion, chopped	1
1/2 tsp	ground ginger	2 mL
2/3 cup	plum sauce	150 mL
2 tbsp	orange juice	25 mL
1/4 tsp	hot pepper sauce	1 mL

● Trim any fat from chops; sprinkle both sides with salt and pepper. In large nonstick skillet, heat oil over medium-high heat; cook chops, turning once, for about 6 minutes or until juices run clear when chops are pierced and just a hint of pink remains inside. Transfer to plate; keep warm.

● Reduce heat to medium. Add red pepper, onion and ginger to pan; cook, stirring occasionally, for about 5 minutes or until onion is softened.

● Stir in plum sauce, orange juice and hot pepper sauce. Return chops and any juices to pan; cook, turning to coat, for about 2 minutes or until heated through. Makes 4 servings.

Red Pepper Pork Chops So-so

Here's a dish that can do double duty in a household — for family and for company. In season, sweet peppers make it very affordable. Round out the menu with buttered pasta and a quick toss of greens.

Per serving: about
- 190 calories
- 9 g fat
- 21 g protein
- 5 g carbohydrate

4	boneless pork chops (1 lb/500 g)	4
1/4 tsp	each salt and pepper	1 mL
1 tbsp	vegetable oil	15 mL
1/3 cup	chopped onion	75 mL
1	clove garlic, minced	1
1/4 tsp	paprika	1 mL
1/2 cup	chicken stock	125 mL
1/4 cup	orange juice	50 mL
2 tsp	cornstarch	10 mL
1/3 cup	roasted sweet red pepper strips	75 mL

● Trim any fat from chops; sprinkle both sides with salt and pepper. In large skillet, heat oil over medium-high heat; brown chops, 3 to 4 minutes per side. Transfer to plate.

● Reduce heat to medium. Add 2 tbsp (25 mL) water to pan, scraping up brown bits. Add onion, garlic and paprika; cook, stirring occasionally, for about 5 minutes or until softened.

● Add stock and orange juice; bring to boil. Dissolve cornstarch in 1 tbsp (15 mL) water; add to pan and cook, stirring, for 1 minute or until thickened. Stir in red pepper strips.

● Return chops to pan along with any accumulated juices. Cook, turning once to coat, for about 3 minutes or until juices run clear when chops are pierced and just a hint of pink remains inside. Makes 4 servings.

VARIATION
● GREEN PEPPER PORK CHOPS: Omit roasted sweet red pepper strips. Thinly slice half of 1 sweet green pepper. Add to pan along with chopped onion; increase cooking time to about 7 minutes.

Herbed Pork Cutlets

1	egg	1
1/3 cup	dry bread crumbs	75 mL
1/4 cup	chopped fresh basil	50 mL
2 tbsp	chopped fresh oregano	25 mL
1 tbsp	freshly grated Parmesan cheese	15 mL
1 tsp	chopped fresh thyme	5 mL
1/2 tsp	pepper	2 mL
1/4 tsp	salt	1 mL
1 lb	fast-fry boneless pork cutlets	500 g
2 tbsp	vegetable oil	25 mL

● In shallow dish, lightly beat egg. In separate shallow dish, stir together bread crumbs, basil, oregano, Parmesan, thyme, pepper and salt. Trim any fat from pork. Dip pork into egg to coat well; press into bread crumb mixture, turning to coat all over.

● In large skillet, heat half of the oil over medium heat; cook pork, in batches and adding remaining oil if necessary, turning once, for 8 to 10 minutes or until juices run clear when pork is pierced and just a hint of pink remains inside. Makes 4 servings.

Fresh herbs are best, but when they're out of season, use dried, cutting amounts to about one-third. Try these quick chops with new potatoes and yellow beans.

Per serving: about
- 255 calories
- 12 g fat
- 28 g protein
- 7 g carbohydrate

Lemony Breaded Pork

1 lb	fast-fry boneless pork cutlets or chops	500 g
1-1/2 tsp	paprika	7 mL
1/2 tsp	dry mustard	2 mL
1/2 tsp	each salt and pepper	2 mL
Pinch	dried thyme	Pinch
1/3 cup	all-purpose flour	75 mL
2	eggs	2
2 cups	fresh bread crumbs	500 mL
2 tbsp	vegetable oil	25 mL
1	lemon, cut in wedges	1

● Trim any fat from pork. Combine paprika, mustard, salt, pepper and thyme. In shallow dish, combine one-third of the paprika mixture with flour. In separate dish, beat together another third of the paprika mixture with eggs. In third dish, combine remaining paprika mixture with bread crumbs.

● Dredge pork in flour mixture, shaking off excess; dip into egg mixture, then into bread crumb mixture, patting firmly onto both sides.

● In large skillet, heat oil over high heat; cook chops, in batches and turning once, for 4 to 6 minutes or until browned and juices run clear when pork is pierced and just a hint of pink remains inside. Squeeze lemon juice over top. Makes 4 servings.

Chicken or turkey cutlets offer an easy alternative to pork cutlets.

Per serving: about
- 395 calories
- 23 g fat
- good source of iron
- 26 g protein
- 20 g carbohydrate

TIP: To dredge, lay the pork cutlets in the flour mixture, pressing gently and turning to coat evenly all over. Shake off excess before continuing with recipe.

Chicken Fried Rice ▶

When what-to-make-for-dinner-tonight starts to hum in your head, turn down the volume and waltz confidently into the kitchen to make this satisfying meal. This family-pleaser is simplicity itself. Round out the menu with a green salad other members of the household can prepare.

Per serving: about
- 445 calories
- 6 g fat
- high source of fiber
- 34 g protein
- 61 g carbohydrate
- good source of iron

TIP: Sesame oil is made from toasted sesame seeds. Its enchanting aroma adds a delicious note to many Asian-style dishes.

1-1/3 cups	long-grain rice	325 mL
1	each onion, carrot and sweet red pepper	1
8 oz	mushrooms	250 g
2	cloves garlic	2
1 lb	boneless skinless chicken breasts	500 g
1 tbsp	sesame or vegetable oil	15 mL
3 tbsp	soy sauce	50 mL
2 tbsp	water	25 mL
1 tbsp	Dijon mustard	15 mL
1 tbsp	chili sauce or ketchup	15 mL
Dash	hot pepper sauce	Dash
1/2 cup	frozen green peas	125 mL

1 In large saucepan, bring 2-2/3 cups (650 mL) water to boil; stir in rice. Reduce heat to low; cover and cook for 20 minutes or until rice is tender and water is absorbed. Meanwhile, chop onion, carrot and red pepper; quarter mushrooms and mince garlic. Set aside separately. Cut chicken into bite-size pieces.

2 In nonstick skillet, heat 1 tsp (5 mL) of the oil over medium-high heat; stir-fry chicken for 5 minutes or until no longer pink inside. Transfer to plate. Add remaining oil to pan; stir-fry onion and garlic for 3 minutes or until softened. Add carrot, red pepper and mushrooms; stir-fry for 8 minutes or until tender.

3 Stir together soy sauce, water, mustard, chili sauce and hot pepper sauce. Stir rice, peas, reserved chicken and any accumulated juices into skillet; pour soy mixture over top. Cook, stirring, until heated through. Makes 4 servings.

FOR GOOD MEASURE

Careful measuring of ingredients is important for best results. Also, be sure you consistently follow either the imperial or the metric system throughout the recipe — never a combination of the two.

● There are two types of measuring cups: dry-ingredient and liquid-ingredient. Dry-ingredient measures come in sets of graduated sizes in imperial (1/4 cup, 1/3 cup, 1/2 cup and 1 cup) and metric (50 mL, 75 mL, 125 mL, 250 mL).

Levels are marked on the outside of liquid-ingredient measures, with enough space below the rim to prevent spills.

● Measuring spoons are used for both dry and liquid ingredients. Imperial measures are 1/4 tsp, 1/2 tsp, 1 tsp, 1 tbsp; metric measures are 1 mL, 2 mL, 5 mL, 15 mL.

Dry Ingredients

● Lightly spoon dry ingredients into dry measure, filling until heaping. Level off by running straight edge of

knife across top. Do not pack or tap measure when filling. (If flour is packed, you could end up with 1/4 cup/50 mL more than called for.) Brown sugar, however, should be packed lightly until it holds the shape of the measure when it is turned out.

Liquid Ingredients

● Place liquid measure on counter; pour in liquid to desired level, bending down to check measurement at eye level and pouring out or adding as necessary.

Fat Ingredients

● For soft fats, press firmly into dry measure, then level off top. For butter and other firm fats, use handy package markings as guides to slice off the amount needed. When there are no markings, use the displacement method:

If a recipe calls for 1/2 cup (125 mL) butter, fill liquid measuring cup with 1/2 cup (125 mL) water; submerge enough butter to make water level rise to 1 cup (250 mL). Drain off water.

Update on Swedish Meatballs ◀ *Excellent*

2 tsp	vegetable oil	10 mL
6 cups	sliced mushrooms (1 lb/500 g)	1.5 L
2 tsp	chopped fresh dill *basil* (or 1/2 tsp/2 mL dried)	10 mL
1/4 tsp	each salt and pepper	1 mL
2/3 cup	2% evaporated milk	150 mL
3 tbsp	rye cracker crumbs	50 mL
3 tbsp	finely chopped onion	50 mL
1/2 tsp	ground allspice } *omit*	2 mL
1/4 tsp	nutmeg	1 mL
12 oz	lean ground beef / *veal*	375 g
4 tsp	all-purpose flour	20 mL
2/3 cup	beef stock	150 mL

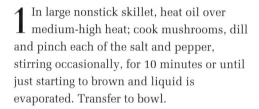

1 In large nonstick skillet, heat oil over medium-high heat; cook mushrooms, dill and pinch each of the salt and pepper, stirring occasionally, for 10 minutes or until just starting to brown and liquid is evaporated. Transfer to bowl.

2 Meanwhile, in separate bowl, combine 2 tbsp (25 mL) of the milk, the cracker crumbs, onion, allspice, nutmeg and remaining salt and pepper; mix in beef. Shape into 1-inch (2.5 cm) balls. Add to skillet; cook, turning often, for 8 minutes or until browned and no longer pink inside.

3 Return mushrooms to skillet; sprinkle with flour and cook, stirring, until absorbed. Pour in stock and remaining milk, stirring and scraping up brown bits; bring to boil. Reduce heat and simmer, stirring occasionally, for 4 minutes or until thickened. Makes 4 servings.

*D*ishes remain classics because they taste good, are easy to make and appeal to lots of palates. This nordic classic is an excellent example that retains all its appeal in spite of a fat-lowering makeover — we used a low-fat evaporated milk instead of whipping cream. This substitution works best in a dish where the cooked-milk taste is masked by other assertive flavors such as mushrooms. Noodles or rice are called for to sop up the creamy mushroom sauce, along with a tangy toss of greens.

Per serving: about
- 295 calories
- 22 g protein
- 17 g fat
- 15 g carbohydrate
- excellent source of iron

TIP: Coordinating the cooking of several dishes at a time is a skill cooks acquire from thinking through each recipe. Here we suggest putting the salted water on to boil before you start the meal so you can stir in the egg noodles when you stir the stock into the skillet for the meatballs. Toss a salad while the meatballs simmer to tasty tenderness.

Thai Chicken Curry ▶

V.G.

For newcomers to cooking Thai at home, ingredients bear some explanation. Thai red curry paste is now available in many major supermarkets. It comes commonly in cans or pouches, and can be fiery hot. Adjust amounts accordingly. Indian curry paste and curry powder are adequate substitutes — the flavor will no longer be Thai, but the taste will be good. Fish sauce looks more like soy sauce than anything else, and it provides saltiness and a funky flavor that mellows as the dish cooks. Store in the refrigerator. Canned coconut milk comes in two versions, regular and light. If the light is not available, stretch 1/2 cup (125 mL) regular coconut milk (which is thicker and 75% higher in fat than light) with the same amount of water. Steamed broccoli spears or coleslaw are good accompaniments to this spicy dish.

Per serving: about
• 470 calories   • 40 g protein
• 9 g fat   • 55 g carbohydrate
• good source
  of iron

1-1/4 cups	basmati rice	300 mL
1-1/4 lb	boneless skinless chicken breasts	625 g
1 tbsp	vegetable oil	15 mL
4 tsp	Thai red curry paste	20 mL
1	onion, coarsely chopped	1
1 tbsp	grated lemon rind	15 mL
1	sweet red pepper, cut in thin strips	1
1 cup	light coconut milk	250 mL
2 tbsp	fish sauce — *like dislike*	25 mL
1 tbsp	lemon juice	15 mL
1/3 cup	chopped fresh coriander	75 mL

↑ I don't like coriander

1 In saucepan, bring 2-2/3 cups (650 mL) salted water to boil; add rice. Reduce heat to low; cover and simmer for 20 minutes or until tender and no liquid remains (or follow cooking instructions on package).

2 Meanwhile, cut chicken into 1/4-inch (5 mm) thick strips. In large nonstick skillet, heat oil over high heat; stir-fry curry paste for 30 seconds. Add chicken; stir-fry for 3 minutes. Add onion; stir-fry for 1 minute.

3 Add lemon rind and red pepper; stir-fry for 1 minute or until onion is softened. Stir in coconut milk, fish sauce and lemon juice; bring to boil and boil for 2 minutes or until liquid is reduced slightly. Stir in coriander. Serve over rice. Makes 4 servings.

Asian Beef and Noodle Stir-Fry ◄

2 tsp	vegetable oil	10 mL
1 tbsp	minced gingerroot	15 mL
1	clove garlic, minced	1
1	onion, sliced	1
1 lb	lean ground beef	500 g
1-1/2 cups	beef stock	375 mL
1/3 cup	oyster sauce	75 mL
2 tbsp	each soy sauce and rice vinegar	25 mL
1 tbsp	packed brown sugar	15 mL
2	carrots, sliced	2
1	pkg (450 g) precooked Chinese noodles	1
1	sweet red pepper, julienned	1
1 tbsp	cornstarch	15 mL
1-1/2 cups	snow peas	375 mL
	Salt and pepper	

1 In wok or large deep skillet, heat oil over high heat; stir-fry ginger, garlic and onion for 30 seconds. Add beef; stir-fry, breaking up meat, for 4 minutes or until no longer pink. Skim off any fat.

2 Stir together stock, oyster sauce, soy sauce, vinegar and sugar; add to wok. Add carrots; bring to boil. Tear noodles apart; add to wok. Cook, stirring, over medium-high heat for 2 minutes. Add red pepper; cook, stirring, for 3 minutes.

3 Dissolve cornstarch in 1 tbsp (15 mL) water; stir into wok and cook, stirring, for 1 minute or until thickened. Stir in snow peas; cook for 2 minutes or until tender-crisp. Season with salt and pepper to taste. Makes 4 servings.

*A*s more quick-cook products are added to supermarket shelves, more and more divine dishes can be made within the 30-minute limit. Thick precooked Chinese noodles sold in vacuum packs in the cooler section of the supermarket are just such a packet of convenience. Serve with a basket of crunchy rice cakes.

Per serving: about
- 665 calories
- 20 g fat
- very high source of fiber
- 38 g protein
- 81 g carbohydrate
- excellent source of iron

TIP: When stir-frying, choose lean beef and drain off fat after browning.

Tomato Beef Stir-Fry ▶

Woks were all the rage a decade ago when Chinese cooking first became fashionable. Then flat-bottomed woks — more like deep skillets than the traditional round-bottom woks — became available and these are now the best choice for stir-frying. However, you can also use a large skillet with high sides or a shallow Dutch oven and enjoy the results as much. Stir-fries and rice are popular plate partners, but consider noodles as a rice alternative — Chinese, if you can find them, but linguine or fettuccine are good substitutes.

Per serving: about
- 190 calories
- 6 g fat
- good source of iron
- 20 g protein
- 15 g carbohydrate

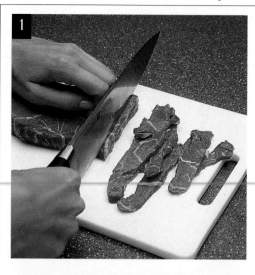

12 oz	lean sirloin steak	375 g
2 tsp	vegetable oil	10 mL
2	onions, sliced lengthwise	2
2	zucchini, sliced	2
Half	sweet red pepper, chopped	Half
1	clove garlic, minced	1
1 tsp	ginger	5 mL
1/2 cup	water	125 mL
3 tbsp	oyster sauce	50 mL
1 tbsp	soy sauce	15 mL
2 tsp	cornstarch	10 mL
1 tsp	vinegar	5 mL
Dash	hot pepper sauce	Dash
2	plum tomatoes, chopped	2

1 Cut beef across the grain into thin strips. In large nonstick skillet or regular wok, heat half of the oil over high heat; stir-fry beef until browned. Transfer to plate.

2 Add remaining oil to pan; stir-fry onions, zucchini, red pepper, garlic and ginger for 1 minute or until slightly softened. Pour in water, stirring and scraping up brown bits; cover and cook for 2 minutes.

3 Stir together oyster sauce, soy sauce, cornstarch, vinegar and hot pepper sauce; pour into pan. Return meat to pan; stir-fry until sauce is thickened and meat mixture is glossy. Add tomatoes; stir to heat through. Makes 4 servings.

TIP: Get the noodles or rice on the go before preparing the ingredients for the stir-fry so they'll both be ready at the same time.

Stir-Fry Tofu and Vegetables

Tofu is a great source of plant protein and is the closest to animal protein in essential amino acids. A regularly stocked item in neighborhood supermarkets, tofu is a very useful ingredient in vegetarian diets.

Per serving: about
- 280 calories
- 12 g fat
- good source of calcium
- 17 g protein
- 27 g carbohydrate
- very high source of fiber

TIP: To use firm instead of extra-firm tofu, wrap it in clean tea towel, place on plate and weigh down with heavy can for 1 hour to press out moisture before cutting into cubes.

1 tbsp	vegetable oil	15 mL
3	cloves garlic, minced	3
1 tbsp	minced gingerroot	15 mL
1/2 tsp	Asian chili paste (or 1/4 tsp/1 mL hot pepper flakes)	2 mL
3	green onions, chopped	3
1 tbsp	black bean sauce (or 2 tbsp/25 mL hoisin sauce)	15 mL
1	onion, sliced	1
2	large carrots, thinly sliced	2
1	each sweet green and red pepper, cut in chunks	1
1-1/2 cups	broccoli florets	375 mL
1/2 cup	vegetable or chicken stock	125 mL
1/4 cup	teriyaki sauce	50 mL
1 tbsp	cornstarch	15 mL
	TOFU	
1	pkg (350 g) extra-firm tofu	1
2 tbsp	each teriyaki sauce and vegetable oil	25 mL

● TOFU: Cut tofu into 1-inch (2.5 cm) chunks; pat dry and place in shallow dish. Sprinkle with teriyaki sauce. Cover and set aside to marinate for 15 minutes or refrigerate for up to 2 hours. In wok or large deep skillet, heat oil over high heat; stir-fry tofu for about 4 minutes or until browned. Transfer to plate.

● Add oil to pan; stir-fry garlic, ginger, chili paste and green onions for about 30 seconds or until fragrant. Stir in black bean sauce. Add onion, carrots, green and red peppers and broccoli; stir-fry for 3 minutes.

● Add stock and teriyaki sauce. Reduce heat to medium-high. Add tofu; cook, stirring occasionally, for 5 minutes. Stir cornstarch into 2 tbsp (25 mL) water; stir into pan and cook, stirring, until thickened. Makes 4 servings.

Ginger Chicken   ~~delicious~~ yuck   (~~Adam didn't like though~~)

Author Anne Lindsay serves this ginger dish with basmati rice and herbed carrots.

Per serving: about
- 190 calories
- 5 g fat
- 28 g protein
- 7 g carbohydrate

1 lb	boneless skinless chicken breasts	500 g
2 tbsp	minced gingerroot	25 mL
2 tbsp	soy sauce	25 mL
1 tbsp	oyster sauce	15 mL
1 tsp	granulated sugar	5 mL
1/2 tsp	cornstarch	2 mL
Pinch	cayenne pepper	Pinch
1 tbsp	vegetable oil	15 mL
2	cloves garlic, minced	2
1 cup	thinly sliced mushrooms	250 mL
1	sweet green or red pepper, cut in thin strips	1
1/4 cup	fresh coriander leaves	50 mL

● Cut chicken across the grain into 1-inch (2.5 cm) thick strips. In small bowl, stir together ginger, soy sauce, oyster sauce, 1 tbsp (15 mL) water, sugar, cornstarch and cayenne; set aside.

● In large nonstick skillet or wok, heat oil over high heat; stir-fry chicken and garlic for 2 minutes. Add mushrooms and green pepper; stir-fry for 1 minute. Add ginger mixture; stir-fry for 1 minute or until thickened and chicken is no longer pink inside. Serve sprinkled with coriander. Makes 4 servings.

Southwestern Stir-Fry with Avocado Salsa V.G.

1 lb	boneless skinless chicken breasts	500 g
4 2 tsp	chili powder	10 mL
3/4 tsp	salt	4 mL
1/2 cup	tomato juice	125 mL
1 tbsp	cornstarch	15 mL
2	corn cobs, husked (or 2 cups/500 mL corn kernels)	2
1	sweet red pepper	1
1	zucchini	1
4 tsp	vegetable oil	20 mL
2	cloves garlic, minced	2
1 tsp	ground cumin	5 mL
1 cup →	cooked black or red kidney beans	250 mL
	AVOCADO SALSA	
1	avocado, peeled and diced	1
2 tbsp	chopped fresh coriander	25 mL
2 tbsp	lime or lemon juice	25 mL

● Cut chicken across the grain into 1/4-inch (5 mm) thick strips. In bowl, toss together chicken, chili powder and salt; set aside. In small bowl, whisk together tomato juice, 1/4 cup (50 mL) water and cornstarch; set aside.

● Cut kernels from corn cobs. Seed and core red pepper; cut into thin 2-inch (5 cm) long strips. Cut zucchini in half lengthwise; cut diagonally into thin slices. Set vegetables aside.

● Heat wok over high heat; add half of the oil, swirling to coat pan. Stir-fry chicken for 2 minutes or until no longer pink inside; transfer to plate.

● Add remaining oil to wok; stir-fry corn, red pepper, zucchini, garlic and cumin for 2 minutes or until corn starts to brown and zucchini is tender-crisp. Add tomato juice mixture; cook, stirring, for about 1 minute or until thickened. Return chicken to pan along with black beans; stir just until coated and steaming. Serve with avocado salsa. Makes 4 servings.

● AVOCADO SALSA: In bowl, combine avocado, coriander and lime juice; set aside.

Just as you don't need a wok to cook Chinese, neither do you need to limit your wok to Asian flavors. Here, a classic stir-fry technique lends itself to Santa Fe seasonings. You can still serve this stir-fry with rice, or try tortillas.

Per serving: about
- 408 calories
- 15 g fat
- very high source of fiber
- 34 g protein
- 38 g carbohydrate
- excellent source of iron

Garden Vegetable Stir-Fry for One

1/2 cup	vegetable, chicken or beef stock	125 mL
1/3 cup	couscous	75 mL
2 tsp	vegetable oil	10 mL
1/4 cup	chopped onion	50 mL
2 tsp	minced gingerroot	10 mL
2 cups	packed fresh spinach, chopped	500 mL
1/2 cup	each diced sweet red and green pepper	125 mL
1/2 cup	sugar snap peas, trimmed	125 mL
Pinch	each salt and pepper	Pinch
2 tsp	soy sauce	10 mL
1/4 cup	sliced radishes	50 mL

● In saucepan, bring stock to boil. Add couscous; cover and remove from heat. Let stand for 5 minutes; fluff with fork.

● Meanwhile, in nonstick skillet, heat oil over medium-high heat; stir-fry onion and ginger for about 3 minutes or until softened.

● Add spinach, red and green peppers, peas, salt and pepper; stir-fry for about 2 minutes or just until spinach is wilted. Drizzle with soy sauce; cover and cook for 1 minute. Fold in couscous and radishes. Makes 1 serving.

This flavorful combo of crunchy vegetables and quick-cooking couscous is a vegetarian entrée for one, but also does nicely as two side dishes. Crunch usually comes from water chestnuts, but here radishes are a tasty substitute.

Per serving: about
- 434 calories
- 11 g fat
- very high source of fiber
- excellent source of iron
- 17 g protein
- 69 g carbohydrate
- good source of calcium

Mango Curried Chicken ◄

4	chicken legs (2 lb/1 kg)	4
1 tbsp	vegetable oil	15 mL
1	onion, chopped	1
2	cloves garlic, minced	2
1	small sweet green pepper, chopped	1
1 cup	long-grain rice	250 mL
2 tsp	curry powder	10 mL
1/2 tsp	each ground cumin and salt	2 mL
1/4 tsp	pepper	1 mL
2 cups	water	500 mL
1/4 cup	mango chutney	50 mL
1 tbsp	tomato paste	15 mL
	Toasted coconut (optional)	

1 Remove skin from chicken. In large nonstick skillet, heat oil over medium-high heat; brown chicken all over, about 10 minutes. Transfer to plate.

2 Drain off all but 2 tsp (10 mL) fat from pan. Add onion, garlic, green pepper, rice, curry powder, cumin, salt and pepper; cook, stirring, for about 3 minutes or just until rice starts to brown. Stir in water, chutney and tomato paste.

3 Nestle chicken in rice mixture; bring to boil. Reduce heat, cover and simmer for 30 to 40 minutes or until juices run clear when chicken is pierced and rice is tender. Serve garnished with coconut (if using). Makes 4 servings.

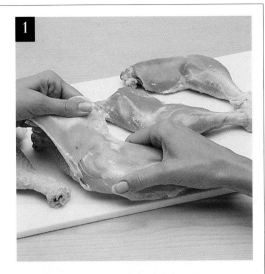

*W*e've stretched the 30 minutes in this recipe, but we haven't stretched the truth about how easy this one-skillet dish is, how healthful it is with only 8 g fat per serving and what a bargain chicken legs are. And we're not exaggerating when we say that it will be a hit with hungry diners. Serve with rice or popadams and a selection of chopped fruit, cucumber, yogurt and chutney.

Per serving: about
- 405 calories
- 31 g protein
- 8 g fat
- 51 g carbohydrate
- good source of iron

TIP: Popadams are thin, crisp Indian breads made from chick-pea flour. To prepare, microwave on High for about 1 minute per popadam, turning halfway, or until puffed and golden.

Hurry Curried Lamb ▶

Lean ground lamb, or beef if you prefer, is the secret to a speedy curry. Serve with sliced cucumbers and radishes in plain yogurt dappled with mint. There are taste rewards when you marry a fragrant curry like this one with basmati rice — and even something as simple as a chopped pear or sliced banana helps round out the meal and the pleasure at the table.

Per serving: about
- 420 calories
- 15 g fat
- very high source of fiber
- 24 g protein
- 61 g carbohydrate
- excellent source of iron

1 tsp	vegetable oil	5 mL
2	onions, chopped	2
2	cloves garlic, minced	2
12 oz	ground lamb or beef	375 g
1 tbsp	curry powder	15 mL
1 tbsp	liquid honey	15 mL
2 tsp	chopped gingerroot	10 mL
1 tsp	ground cumin	5 mL
1/4 tsp	each ground coriander, salt and pepper	1 mL
1	carrot, sliced	1
1	sweet green pepper, cut in chunks	1
1	can (19 oz/540 mL) chick-peas, drained and rinsed	1
1	can (19 oz/540 mL) tomatoes, chopped	1
1/2 cup	raisins	125 mL

1 In large nonstick skillet, heat oil over medium heat; cook onions and garlic, stirring occasionally, for 5 minutes or until softened. Add lamb; cook, breaking up with spoon, for 5 minutes or until no longer pink.

2 Drain off fat. Stir in curry powder, honey, ginger, cumin, coriander, salt and pepper. Stir in carrot, green pepper, chick-peas, tomatoes and juices and raisins; bring to boil.

3 Reduce heat to low; cook, stirring occasionally, for 20 minutes or until vegetables are tender and sauce is thickened slightly. Makes 4 servings.

Picadillo

This Latin-American meat hash with vegetables is delicious over rice or rolled up in a tortilla.

Per serving: about
- 265 calories
- 10 g fat
- high source of fiber
- 20 g protein
- 27 g carbohydrate
- excellent source of iron

1 lb	lean ground beef	500 g
2	onions, chopped	2
4	cloves garlic, minced	4
2	small sweet green peppers, chopped	2
1	can (5-1/2 oz/156 mL) tomato paste	1
1 cup	water	250 mL
1/2 cup	raisins	125 mL
1/4 cup	chopped pitted green olives	50 mL
2 tbsp	capers, drained	25 mL
2 tbsp	Worcestershire sauce	25 mL
2 tbsp	red wine vinegar	25 mL
1/4 tsp	each salt and pepper	1 mL

● In large nonstick skillet, brown beef over medium heat, breaking up with spoon, about 6 minutes. Skim off any fat.

● Add onions; cook, stirring often, for 5 minutes. Add garlic and green peppers; cook, stirring often, for 2 to 3 minutes or until onions are softened.

● Mix tomato paste with water; stir into beef mixture. Stir in raisins, olives, capers and Worcestershire sauce; simmer for 5 minutes. Stir in vinegar, salt and pepper. Makes 5 servings.

Cajun Rice and Beans ◀

2 tsp	vegetable oil	10 mL
1/2 cup	diced cooked ham	125 mL
2	cloves garlic, minced	2
1	red onion, chopped	1
3/4 cup	diced seeded peeled tomato	175 mL
Half	sweet green or red pepper, chopped	Half
3/4 cup	corn kernels	175 mL
1	bay leaf	1
1/4 cup	chopped fresh parsley	50 mL
1/2 tsp	salt	2 mL
1/4 tsp	each hot pepper flakes and pepper	1 mL
1 cup	water	250 mL
2 cups	cooked or canned red kidney beans, drained and rinsed	500 mL
2 cups	hot cooked long-grain brown rice	500 mL
1/4 cup	thinly sliced green onions	50 mL

● In saucepan, heat oil over medium heat; cook ham, garlic and onion, stirring often, for 5 minutes.

● Add tomato, green pepper, corn, bay leaf, parsley, salt, hot pepper flakes and pepper. Stir in water; bring to boil. Reduce heat and simmer for 2 minutes.

● Crush half of the beans; stir crushed and whole beans into pan. Cook, stirring often, for 10 minutes. Discard bay leaf. Serve over rice; garnish with green onions. Makes 4 servings.

Lusty spices and robust tastes, both characteristics of Louisiana cooking, add zest to home cooking. For a vegetarian version, omit the ham.

Per serving: about
- 348 calories
- 5 g fat
- very high source of fiber
- 17 g protein
- 61 g carbohydrate
- excellent source source of iron

Curried Vegetables

2	carrots, thickly sliced	2
2	potatoes, cut in small chunks	2
2 cups	cauliflower florets	500 mL
1 tbsp	vegetable oil	15 mL
2	onions, chopped	2
1 tsp	each curry powder, ground cumin, turmeric and mustard seeds	5 mL
1/2 tsp	each salt and hot pepper flakes	2 mL
1/4 tsp	cinnamon	1 mL
1	can (19 oz/540 mL) tomatoes, chopped	1

● In saucepan of boiling salted water, cover and cook carrots and potatoes for 5 minutes. Add cauliflower; cook for 5 minutes. Drain and set aside.

● In large heavy saucepan, heat oil over medium heat; cook onions, stirring occasionally, for 3 to 4 minutes or until softened. Stir in curry powder, cumin, turmeric, mustard seeds, salt, hot pepper flakes and cinnamon; cook for 1 minute or until mustard seeds begin to pop.

● Add tomatoes and 1/2 cup (125 mL) water, scraping up brown bits from bottom of pan; bring to boil. Stir in carrot mixture. Reduce heat to medium-low; cover and simmer for 5 minutes. Makes 4 servings.

Almost any vegetable can be curried so don't feel limited by the selection here. Serve over steaming rice and offer little bowls of condiments — chopped apple, chopped nuts, toasted coconut, thick yogurt and, of course, chutney.

Per serving: about
- 175 calories
- 5 g fat
- high source of fiber
- 5 g protein
- 32 g carbohydrate
- good source of iron

Sandwiches, Burgers & Wraps

Tortilla Sandwich Melts ▶

Dense but thin, tortillas are a terrific alternative to bread. In addition to their many uses, they are perfect for fold-over melt sandwiches (quesadillas). You can make these supper sandwiches in the oven, on a griddle, in a heavy skillet or, as in this recipe, on the barbecue. Salads are always a good contrast to cheese-based dishes, and these quesadillas are no exception. Start with lettuce and tomatoes, then add according to what you have in the crisper.

Per serving: about
- 480 calories
- 23 g protein
- 17 g fat
- 60 g carbohydrate
- very high source of fiber
- excellent source of calcium and iron

1	can (19 oz/540 mL) kidney beans, drained and rinsed	1
1 cup	salsa	250 mL
4	flour tortillas (10-inch/25 cm)	4
4	green onions, chopped	4
1/4 cup	chopped green olives	50 mL
2 tbsp	chopped fresh coriander or parsley	25 mL
1-1/3 cups	shredded extra-old Cheddar cheese	325 mL

1 In bowl and using potato masher, mash beans with 1/2 cup (125 mL) of the salsa.

2 Divide bean mixture among tortillas, spreading evenly and leaving 1/2-inch (1 cm) border. Sprinkle with onions, then olives; sprinkle with coriander, then cheese. Fold tortillas over and press gently.

3 Place on greased grill over medium-high heat; close lid and cook, turning once, for 8 to 10 minutes or until browned and crisped. Garnish with remaining salsa. Makes 4 servings.

TIP: For a stringier cheese, try Monterey Jack. You might also like Danbo, a lower-fat cheese that has lots of flavor.

QUESADILLAS FOR EVERY TASTE

For a quick and casual meal any time of the year, nothing beats a platter assortment of quesadilla wedges.
Choose the method of cooking that suits the season, and offer Salsa Ranchero (or your favorite store-bought salsa) for dipping.
Round out the meal with a big bowlful of crisp greens.

VEGGIE QUESADILLAS

1	sweet red pepper	1
3	small zucchini	3
1 tbsp	olive oil	15 mL
1-1/2 tsp	finely chopped fresh rosemary	7 mL
1/4 tsp	each salt and pepper	1 mL
4 oz	cream goat cheese (chèvre)	125 g
6	flour tortillas (7-inch/18 cm)	6

● Halve, core and seed red pepper; broil, cut side down, on lightly greased baking sheet for about 15 minutes or until blackened. Let cool for 10 minutes. Peel off charred skin; cut into thin strips.

● Cut zucchini in half crosswise; cut lengthwise into thin slices and place on baking sheet. Stir together oil, rosemary, salt and pepper; brush over zucchini. Broil for about 8 minutes or until softened. Let cool. *(Vegetables can be covered and refrigerated for up to 8 hours.)*

● Spread cheese evenly over tortillas, leaving 1/2-inch (1 cm) border. Arrange zucchini and peppers over bottom half of each. Fold tortilla over and press gently. Cook (see Cooking Quesadillas); let stand for 5 minutes before cutting each into 3 wedges. Makes 18 wedges.

Per wedge: about • 63 calories • 2 g protein • 3 g fat • 8 g carbohydrate

CHICK-PEA QUESADILLAS

1	can (19 oz/540 mL) chick-peas, drained and rinsed	1
2 tbsp	extra virgin olive oil	25 mL
1/2 cup	diced sweet red pepper	125 mL
2	green onions, chopped	2
3 tbsp	chopped fresh coriander or parsley	50 mL
1 tsp	lemon juice	5 mL
1/2 tsp	each dried oregano and salt	2 mL
1/2 tsp	hot pepper sauce	2 mL
6	flour tortillas (7-inch/18 cm)	6

● In food processor, combine chick-peas with oil until chunky paste forms; transfer to bowl. Add red pepper, onions, coriander, lemon juice, oregano, salt and hot pepper sauce; stir until combined. *(Filling can be covered and refrigerated for up to 8 hours.)*

● Divide chick-pea mixture among tortillas, spreading over half of each and leaving 1/2-inch (1 cm) border. Fold tortilla over filling and press gently. Cook (see Cooking Quesadillas); let stand for 5 minutes before cutting each into 3 wedges. Makes 18 wedges.

Per wedge: about • 77 calories • 3 g protein • 3 g fat • 11 g carbohydrate

SALSA RANCHERO

1/2 tsp	dried oregano	2 mL
1/2 tsp	ground cumin	2 mL
1	large jalapeño pepper	1
Half	sweet yellow pepper	Half
1	large tomato	1
Half	small white onion	Half
2	cloves garlic	2
2 tbsp	chopped fresh coriander	25 mL
1 tbsp	olive oil	15 mL
	Salt	

● In heavy skillet, heat oregano and cumin over medium-low heat for 2 minutes or until fragrant; transfer to bowl. Chop and seed jalapeño and yellow peppers; add to bowl.

● Chop tomato, onion and garlic; add to bowl along with coriander, oil, and salt to taste. Makes 3 cups (750 mL).

Per 1/2 cup (125 mL): about • 36 calories • 1 g protein • 3 g fat • 4 g carbohydrate

COOKING QUESADILLAS

● **Stovetop:** Heat nonstick skillet over medium heat. Cook tortillas, 2 at a time and turning halfway through, for about 4 minutes or until filling is piping hot.

● **Oven:** Place on baking sheet; bake in 400°F (200°C) oven, turning halfway through, for about 8 minutes or until filling is piping hot.

● **Grill:** Place on lightly greased grill over medium heat; close lid and cook, turning halfway through, for about 8 minutes or until filling is piping hot.

Barbecued Quesadillas

1	small avocado	1
1	tomato, diced	1
1/2 cup	corn kernels	125 mL
1/4 cup	chopped canned green chilies or green onion	50 mL
1/4 tsp	salt	1 mL
Pinch	pepper	Pinch
8	flour tortillas (8-inch/20 cm)	8
1 cup	shredded part-skim mozzarella cheese	250 mL
1/3 cup	chopped fresh coriander or parsley	75 mL

● Peel and pit avocado. In small bowl, mash half of the avocado. Chop remaining half; stir into mashed avocado. Stir in tomato, corn, green chilies, salt and pepper.

● Divide avocado mixture among tortillas, spreading over half of each and leaving 1/2-inch (1 cm) border uncovered. Sprinkle with cheese and coriander; fold tortilla over filling and press gently.

● Place on greased grill over medium heat or in nonstick skillet; close lid and cook, turning once, for about 3 minutes or until lightly browned and cheese is melted. Makes 8 quesadillas.

Serve these melty Mexican-inspired quesadillas for supper or for a hearty snack. Note that for a snack, one quesadilla is enough, but for a meal, you will need two.

Per quesadilla: about
- 230 calories
- 9 g protein
- 9 g fat
- 30 g carbohydrate
- good source of calcium

Fresh Coleslaw Reubens

4	slices rye bread	4
2 tsp	sweet mustard	10 mL
2	slices light Swiss-style or Cheddar-style cheese	2
2 oz	shaved corned beef	60 g
	SLAW	
1 cup	finely shredded cabbage	250 mL
1	carrot, shredded	1
2 tbsp	cider vinegar	25 mL
1 tbsp	vegetable oil	15 mL
4 tsp	granulated sugar	20 mL
Pinch	each celery seed, salt and pepper	Pinch

● SLAW: In small bowl, combine cabbage with carrot; set aside. In small saucepan, combine vinegar, oil, sugar, celery seed, salt and pepper; bring to boil. Pour over cabbage mixture and stir; let stand for 10 minutes.

● Meanwhile, heat sandwich maker; spray lightly with cooking spray. Trim bread slices to fit sandwich maker if necessary; spread 1 side of each with mustard. Top 2 of the slices with cheese, then corned beef. Using slotted spoon, top each with 2 tbsp (25 mL) slaw. Top with remaining bread.

● Place in sandwich maker and lock lid; cook for about 3 minutes or until golden and filling is hot. Let cool slightly. Serve with remaining slaw. Makes 2 servings.

In the world of suppers, you can't be a snob and rule out sandwiches, especially if you make them hot — on the griddle, in the oven or in a sandwich maker.

Per serving: about
- 416 calories
- 20 g protein
- 18 g fat
- 45 g carbohydrate
- good source of iron
- excellent source of calcium

TIPS

● If you don't have a sandwich maker, butter outsides of bread with 2 tsp (10 mL) butter; cook in nonstick skillet over medium heat for 3 to 5 minutes per side or until cheese is melted.

● There's enough coleslaw for the sandwiches and side helpings. Or, save the extra slaw for tomorrow's lunch.

GOOD-FOR-YOU SWEET ENDINGS

The quick desserts below all add real food value to any meal and many are based on fresh fruit — fruit that's usually no more expensive than most commercial baked goods, especially when it's in season and locally produced.

● **Bananas** are the best bargain available, and enjoyable out of hand, or sliced over a yogurt sundae sprinkled with toasted pecans.

● **Easy-to-peel clementines and mandarins** star among citrus fruit. Sprinkle with chopped mint or dust with cinnamon.

● **Berries,** especially fresh local strawberries, raspberries, blueberries and blackberries. Drizzle with frozen raspberry or orange juice concentrate and add a dollop of thick yogurt.

● **Melon:** Cantaloupe is the most reliable year round, especially in July and August when Canadian melons are

available. Serve in wedges with a dash of ginger or wedge of lime.

● **Peaches, nectarines, cherries and plums** in season make a splendid dessert. In cold weather, look for mangos, already peeled pineapple, kiwi and papaya.

● **Fruit sorbets or gelati** are

unbelievably good alone, in combination and with or without fresh fruit or fruit syrups. Try lighter frozen yogurts, frozen yogurt with sorbets and ice milk, too.

● **Yogurt:** Try the plain low-fat vanilla yogurt with fruit, a drizzle of maple syrup or honey or a sprinkle of low-fat granola.

Grilled Sausage Sandwiches ◄

1 tbsp	olive oil	15 mL
1	onion, chopped	1
1	clove garlic, minced	1
1	sweet red pepper, coarsely chopped	1
Pinch	hot pepper flakes	Pinch
1	can (19 oz/540 mL) Italian Spice Stewed Tomatoes	1
2 tbsp	chopped fresh parsley	25 mL
1/4 tsp	each salt and pepper	1 mL
4	Italian sausages (about 1 lb/500 g)	4
4	crusty Italian rolls	4
4	lettuce leaves	4
4 tsp	freshly grated Parmesan cheese	20 mL

1 In saucepan, heat oil over medium heat; cook onion and garlic, stirring occasionally, for 5 minutes or until softened. Add red pepper and hot pepper flakes; cook for 2 minutes. Stir in tomatoes, parsley, salt and pepper; bring to boil. Reduce heat and simmer for 20 minutes or until thickened.

2 Meanwhile, cut sausages lengthwise almost all the way through. Open and place, cut side down, on greased grill over medium-high heat; close lid and cook, turning once, for about 10 minutes or until no longer pink inside.

3 Cut rolls in half lengthwise; toast, cut side down, for 2 to 3 minutes or just until golden. Top each bottom half with lettuce and sausage; spoon tomato sauce over top. Sprinkle with Parmesan cheese; cover with top half of roll. Makes 4 servings.

TIP: You can adjust the spiciness of this hearty main-course sandwich from mild to frisky by using either sweet or hot sausages.

*W*inter or summer, spring or fall, there's a welcome mat out for this kind of sandwich supper. The sausage is the star, but it needs the zesty tomato sauce and toasted torpedo buns to make the package so desirable — and so hard to eat daintily! Enjoy outdoors whenever possible, and provide enough napkins to keep the ruby red tomato sauce off ties and tops.

Per serving: about
- 505 calories
- 22 g fat
- high source of fiber
- 26 g protein
- 52 g carbohydrate
- excellent source of iron

Beef Kibbe Patties ▶

These Middle East-inspired patties feature the same intriguing combination of meat, cracked wheat and cinnamon that is found in traditional Lebanese kibbe but are much quicker to make. Serve in warm whole grain pita breads, along with a crisp salad of cucumbers and lettuce tossed with a lemon dressing that's been accented with chopped fresh mint.

Per serving: about
- 330 calories
- 20 g fat
- high source of fiber
- 22 g protein
- 17 g carbohydrate
- good source of iron

TIP: You can reduce the fat by using lean ground beef.

1/2 cup	bulgur	125 mL
1	small onion, finely chopped	1
2 tbsp	pine nuts or chopped almonds	25 mL
2 tbsp	lemon juice	25 mL
1 tsp	each salt and cinnamon	5 mL
1/2 tsp	cayenne pepper (optional)	2 mL
1 lb	ground beef	500 g
	Plain yogurt (optional)	

1 In bowl, cover bulgur with boiling water; let soak for 10 minutes. Drain in sieve, pressing to squeeze out water.

2 In bowl, combine bulgur, onion, pine nuts, lemon juice, salt, cinnamon, and cayenne (if using); mix in beef. Shape into eight 1/2-inch (1 cm) thick patties.

3 In nonstick skillet, cook patties over medium heat, in batches if necessary and turning once, for about 8 minutes or until no longer pink inside. Serve with yogurt (if using). Makes 4 servings.

Bean Burgers with Coriander Cream

1	can (19 oz/540 mL) red kidney beans, drained and rinsed	1
1/2 cup	dry bread crumbs	125 mL
1/2 cup	salsa	125 mL
2 tsp	vegetable oil	10 mL
1/3 cup	light sour cream	75 mL
2 tbsp	minced fresh coriander	25 mL

● In bowl, mash beans with potato masher or fork until fairly smooth but still with some small lumps. Stir in bread crumbs and salsa to make fairly firm mixture. With wet hands, form into four 1/2-inch (1 cm) thick patties.

● In large nonstick skillet, heat oil over medium-high heat; cook patties, turning once, for about 10 minutes or until crusty outside and piping hot inside.

● Meanwhile, stir sour cream with coriander. Serve over patties. Makes 4 servings.

B*ean burgers are just as easy to slap together as many meat patties and go just as well with shredded lettuce, diced avocado and tomatoes.*

Per serving: about
- 220 calories
- 4 g fat
- very high source of fiber
- 11 g protein
- 34 g carbohydrate

Pita Burgers with Mint

Juicy beef patties with a quick minty yogurt sauce nestle nicely in pita pockets. Raw carrot sticks and broccoli florets suit this hands-on casual supper.

Per serving: about
• 425 calories   • 31 g protein
• 16 g fat   • 40 g carbohydrate
• excellent source of iron

1	egg	1
1	small onion, finely chopped	1
2 tbsp	red wine vinegar	25 mL
1 tsp	dried oregano	5 mL
1/2 tsp	each salt and pepper	2 mL
1/4 tsp	cinnamon	1 mL
1 lb	lean ground beef	500 g
1 tbsp	vegetable oil	15 mL
4	small pita breads	4
4	leaves leaf lettuce	4
Half	cucumber, thinly sliced	Half
	YOGURT MINT SAUCE	
2/3 cup	extra-thick plain yogurt	150 mL
2 tbsp	chopped fresh mint	25 mL
1	clove garlic, minced	1
1-1/2 tsp	lemon juice	7 mL

● In bowl, lightly beat egg; mix in onion, vinegar, oregano, salt, pepper and cinnamon. Mix in beef. Shape into eight 1/2-inch (1 cm) thick patties.

● In large nonstick skillet, heat oil over medium heat; cook patties, in batches if necessary and turning once, for about 8 minutes or until no longer pink inside.

● YOGURT MINT SAUCE: Meanwhile, in small bowl, stir together yogurt, mint, garlic and lemon juice.

● Slice off top third of each pita bread; open larger piece to form pocket. Insert top piece, cut side up, into pocket to strengthen bottom. Place 2 patties in each pocket along with lettuce leaf and cucumber; spoon 1 tbsp (15 mL) sauce into each. Serve remaining sauce separately. Makes 4 servings.

TIP: If extra-thick yogurt is unavailable, prepare your own by using drained yogurt. Place 1-1/3 cups (325 mL) plain yogurt in cheesecloth-lined sieve set over bowl. Refrigerate for 3 to 4 hours or overnight or until yogurt is reduced to about 2/3 cup (150 mL).

Oregano Lemon Pork Burgers

Grated onion adds a subtle flavor to these scrumptious burgers. Serve on a crusty roll with sliced tomatoes and prepared tzatziki.

Per serving: about
• 268 calories   • 22 g protein
• 16 g fat   • 7 g carbohydrate

1	small onion, grated	1
1/4 cup	dry bread crumbs	50 mL
2 tbsp	water	25 mL
1 tbsp	chopped fresh oregano	15 mL
2 tsp	grated lemon rind	10 mL
1/4 tsp	each salt and pepper	1 mL
1 lb	lean ground pork	500 g
6	crusty rolls	6

● In bowl, mix together onion, bread crumbs, water, oregano, lemon rind, salt and pepper; mix in pork. Shape into four 3/4-inch (2 cm) thick patties.

● Place on greased grill over medium-high heat or under broiler; close lid and cook, turning once, for about 12 minutes or until no longer pink inside. Sandwich in crusty rolls. Makes 4 servings.

TIP: You can also make these burgers with lean ground beef, chicken or turkey.

Sassy Horseradish Burgers

1	egg	1
1	clove garlic, minced	1
1/4 cup	dry bread crumbs	50 mL
1/4 cup	seafood sauce	50 mL
1	small onion, grated	1
1 tbsp	horseradish	15 mL
1/2 tsp	salt	2 mL
1/4 tsp	pepper	1 mL
1 lb	lean ground beef	500 g
6	hamburger buns	6

● In bowl, lightly beat egg; mix in garlic, bread crumbs, seafood sauce, onion, horseradish, salt and pepper. Mix in beef. Shape into six 3/4-inch (2 cm) thick patties.

● Place on greased grill over medium-high heat; close lid and cook, turning once, for about 12 minutes or until no longer pink inside. Sandwich in buns. Makes 6 servings.

The sass comes from the horseradish. Top with grilled onions, extra seafood or chili sauce.

Per serving: about
- 360 calories
- 21 g protein
- 13 g fat
- 39 g carbohydrate
- good source of iron

Couscous and Chick-Pea Burgers

1 cup	vegetable stock	250 mL
1/2 cup	couscous	125 mL
1 tsp	dried basil	5 mL
3/4 tsp	grated lemon rind	4 mL
1	can (19 oz/540 mL) chick-peas, drained	1
1/3 cup	chopped green onions	75 mL
1	egg	1
2 tbsp	water	25 mL
1	clove garlic, minced	1
1/4 tsp	each salt and pepper	1 mL
1 tsp	vegetable oil	5 mL
2	whole wheat pita breads	2
1/2 cup	light sour cream	125 mL
2 cups	shredded lettuce	500 mL
1/2 cup	sliced cucumber	125 mL
1/4 cup	sliced radishes	50 mL

● In saucepan, bring stock to boil. Remove from heat; stir in couscous, basil and lemon rind. Cover and let stand for 5 minutes. Fluff with fork.

● In food processor, chop chick-peas finely. Add couscous mixture, onions, egg, water, garlic, salt and pepper; pulse until combined. Shape into four 1/2-inch (1 cm) thick patties. *(Patties can be wrapped in plastic wrap and refrigerated in airtight container for up to 8 hours or frozen for up to 2 weeks.)*

● In nonstick skillet, heat oil over medium-high heat; cook patties, turning once, for 8 to 10 minutes or until golden.

● Cut each pita bread in half; open to form pocket. Spread inside with sour cream; fill evenly with patty, lettuce, cucumber and radishes. Makes 4 servings.

If you enjoy falafels — deep-fried savory chick-pea balls — you'll enjoy this baked version.

Per serving: about
- 372 calories
- 17 g protein
- 7 g fat
- 62 g carbohydrate
- very high source of fiber
- good source of iron

FOOD PREPARATION

When handling chicken or other raw meat or fish, always wash your hands before and after. Use hot sudsy water to wash all utensils and pans that held raw product and rinse well with hot water before air drying. Some experts also recommend adding 1 tbsp (15 mL) chlorine bleach per 16 cups (4 L) water when washing up.

Chicken Roll-Ups ◀

4	slices gingerroot	4
1	slice lemon	1
1	clove garlic, sliced	1
1 lb	boneless skinless chicken breasts	500 g
8	leaves leaf lettuce	8
1/2 cup	grated radishes	125 mL
1/2 cup	grated carrots	125 mL
1/2 cup	diced cucumber	125 mL
1/2 cup	bean sprouts	125 mL
	Chopped fresh coriander or basil (optional)	
	SAUCE	
2 tbsp	cornstarch	25 mL
1/2 cup	granulated sugar	125 mL
1 cup	chopped sweet red pepper	250 mL
1/3 cup	lemon juice	75 mL
3 tbsp	soy sauce	50 mL
2	cloves garlic, minced	2
1/2 tsp	hot pepper sauce	2 mL

1 In small skillet, bring 1-1/2 cups (375 mL) water, ginger, lemon and garlic to boil. Add chicken; reduce heat, cover and simmer, turning once, for 10 minutes or just until no longer pink inside. Transfer chicken to plate; let cool. Strain poaching liquid and return to skillet.

2 SAUCE: Dissolve cornstarch in 2 tbsp (25 mL) water; whisk into poaching liquid along with sugar. Bring to boil; cook for 2 minutes or until slightly thickened. Remove from heat. Stir in red pepper, lemon juice, soy sauce, garlic and hot pepper sauce.

3 Shred chicken; toss with 1/2 cup (125 mL) of the sauce. To serve, let each person top lettuce leaf with chicken, radishes, carrots, cucumber, bean sprouts, and coriander (if using); drizzle with some of the remaining sauce. Roll up leaf. Makes 4 servings.

Here's a fast, fun, eat-with-your-hands meal that makes the most of market-fresh fare. It's a healthful meal, too — the raw vegetables retain maximum nutrient value and the poached chicken is low-fat, moist and tender. The zing comes from Vietnamese-inspired sweet-and-sour sauce for dipping. Serve with steamed rice.

Per serving: about
- 280 calories
- 2 g fat
- 28 g protein
- 38 g carbohydrate

TIP: Get the kids to help make supper. They can grate the vegetables and spin-dry the lettuce.

Exotic Sloppy Joes ▶

*F*rom Armenia comes the inspiration for these beef-and-tomato-filled wrappers. The allspice and paprika seasonings, crumbled feta topping and hot pickled peppers make these sandwiches unusual but very tasty. Any plain salad will complement the multitude of flavors in the wrap supper.

Per serving: about
- 610 calories
- 24 g fat
- high source of fiber
- 35 g protein
- 65 g carbohydrate
- excellent source of calcium and iron

1 tsp	vegetable oil	5 mL
1	onion, chopped	1
2	cloves garlic, minced	2
1 tsp	paprika	5 mL
3/4 tsp	ground allspice	4 mL
1/2 tsp	each salt and pepper	2 mL
1 lb	lean ground beef	500 g
1	can (14 oz/398 mL) tomatoes	1
1/4 cup	tomato paste	50 mL
1	sweet green pepper, chopped	1
1/2 cup	chopped fresh parsley	125 mL
8	flour tortillas (8-inch/20 cm), warmed	8
1 cup	diced cucumber	250 mL
1 cup	crumbled feta cheese	250 mL
1/4 cup	hot pickled pepper (optional)	50 mL

1 In nonstick skillet, heat oil over medium-high heat; cook onion and garlic, stirring often, for 3 minutes. Add paprika, allspice, salt and pepper; cook, stirring, for 1 minute. Add beef; cook, breaking up with spoon, for 5 minutes or until no longer pink. Drain off any fat.

2 Add tomatoes and tomato paste, breaking up tomatoes with fork; bring to boil. Reduce heat to medium. Add green pepper and parsley; cook, stirring often, for 10 to 15 minutes or until most of the liquid is evaporated.

3 Divide beef mixture among tortillas; fold tortillas in half to form pockets. Sprinkle filling with cucumber, feta cheese, and pickled pepper (if using). Serve warm. Makes 4 servings.

Chicken Burritos ▲

Making something that everyone in the family will enjoy brings a lot of pleasure to the cook. Here's that kind of dish. Serve it with chopped tomatoes and sour cream.

Per serving: about
- 455 calories
- 13 g fat
- high source of fiber
- excellent source of iron
- 37 g protein
- 48 g carbohydrate
- good source of calcium

1 tbsp	vegetable oil	15 mL
1 lb	boneless skinless chicken breasts, cubed	500 g
1/4 tsp	each salt and pepper	1 mL
1	onion, chopped	1
1	sweet green pepper, diced	1
3/4 cup	salsa	175 mL
1 cup	corn kernels	250 mL
4	flour tortillas (10-inch/25 cm), warmed	4
1/2 cup	shredded Monterey Jack cheese	125 mL

● In large nonstick skillet, heat 1 tsp (5 mL) of the oil over medium-high heat. Sprinkle chicken with salt and pepper; cook, stirring and using up to 1 tsp (5 mL) more oil if necessary, for 5 minutes or until browned and no longer pink inside. Transfer to plate.

● Reduce heat to medium. Add remaining oil to skillet; cook onion and green pepper, stirring occasionally, for 5 minutes or until softened, adding up to 1 tbsp (15 mL) water if necessary to prevent burning.

● Add salsa to pan and bring to boil; reduce heat and simmer, stirring often, for about 3 minutes or until most of the liquid is evaporated. Stir in corn and chicken. Spoon onto tortillas. Sprinkle with cheese and roll up. Makes 4 servings.

Portobello Wraps

1	can (19 oz/540 mL) white kidney beans, drained and rinsed	1
2 tbsp	lemon juice	25 mL
3/4 tsp	salt	4 mL
1/2 tsp	pepper	2 mL
1/2 cup	oil-packed sun-dried tomatoes	125 mL
2 tbsp	chopped fresh basil or oregano	25 mL
1 lb	portobello mushrooms	500 g
1	onion, thinly sliced	1
1	clove garlic, minced	1
1	small zucchini, sliced	1
4	flour tortillas (10-inch/25 cm)	4

● In food processor, purée together beans, lemon juice and 1/4 tsp (1 mL) each salt and pepper; place in bowl. Drain tomatoes, reserving 1 tbsp (15 mL) oil; chop and add to bowl. Add half of the basil. Stem mushrooms; cut into 1/4-inch (5 mm) thick slices. Set aside.

● In nonstick skillet, heat 2 tsp (10 mL) of the reserved oil over medium heat; cook onion and garlic, stirring occasionally, for 5 minutes. Add zucchini, 1/4 tsp (1 mL) salt and remaining pepper; cook for 3 minutes. Transfer to plate; keep warm.

● Heat remaining oil over medium-high heat; cook mushrooms with remaining salt, stirring occasionally, for 7 minutes. Add to zucchini; add remaining basil.

● Spread bean mixture over tortillas, leaving 1-inch (2.5 cm) border; cover lower third with vegetable mixture. Fold bottom border over filling, then sides; roll up. Makes 4 servings.

Portobellos are the giants of the mushroom world. With caps 4 to 6 inches (10 to 15 cm) wide, they are actually cremini mushrooms — the brown version of regular white agaricus mushrooms — that are grown about three days longer before harvesting.

Per serving: about
- 385 calories
- 10 g fat
- very high source of fiber
- 15 g protein
- 63 g carbohydrate
- excellent source of iron

Instant Egg Fajita for One

1/2 tsp	vegetable oil	2 mL
1	green onion, sliced	1
1	egg, beaten	1
Pinch	each salt and pepper	Pinch
1	flour tortilla (8-inch/20 cm)	1
2 tbsp	salsa	25 mL
2 tbsp	shredded Monterey Jack cheese	25 mL
	Strips sweet red or green pepper	

● In nonstick skillet, heat oil over medium heat; cook onion for about 2 minutes or until softened. Reduce heat to low. Pour in egg, rotating skillet to coat bottom; cook for 3 to 4 minutes or until completely set. Sprinkle with salt and pepper. Remove from pan; cut into strips.

● Microwave tortilla at High for 5 seconds. (Or warm in 350°F/180°C oven for 2 minutes.) Place egg strips along center. Top with salsa, cheese and red pepper strips. Fold up bottom over filling, then sides. Makes 1 serving.

When you're looking for speedy preparation, whether for breakfast, lunch or dinner, eggs are a satisfying solution. Try this simple omelette wrapped in a tortilla and see how versatile eggs are with a spiced-up Mexican topping. Garnish with crunchies such as grated carrot or shredded lettuce.

Per serving: about
- 297 calories
- 15 g fat
- good source of calcium and iron
- 14 g protein
- 27 g carbohydrate

Grills and Roasts

Moroccan Chicken with Couscous ▶

Some foods take so little time to cook, you hardly have time to appreciate the aromas. Chicken under the broiler and couscous fit into this quick-cook list but, here, the aroma of sweet Moroccan spices — cumin, coriander, paprika and mint — lets you know just what a feast awaits you. Pair the chicken with shredded zucchini added to couscous as it rehydrates in boiling stock and in minutes you have a meal on the table that everyone will rave about. Toss some tender greens with a dash of dressing to complete the main course.

Per serving: about
- 460 calories
- 12 g fat
- high source of fiber
- 34 g protein
- 53 g carbohydrate
- good source of iron

TIP: Set the rack in your oven so the top of the chicken is about 4 inches (10 cm) from the source of heat.

1/2 cup	orange juice	125 mL
3 tbsp	olive oil	50 mL
1 tbsp	liquid honey	15 mL
3/4 tsp	each ground cumin and coriander	4 mL
3/4 tsp	salt	4 mL
1/2 tsp	each cinnamon, paprika and dried mint	2 mL
1/2 tsp	pepper	2 mL
4	boneless skinless chicken breasts (1 lb/500 g)	4
2	cloves garlic, minced	2
1	small onion, chopped	1
1/4 cup	diced dried apricots	50 mL
1 cup	couscous	250 mL
1	zucchini (4 oz/125 g), shredded	1

1 In small bowl, whisk together 1 tsp (5 mL) of the orange juice, 2 tbsp (25 mL) of the oil, honey, cumin, coriander, 1/4 tsp (1 mL) of the salt, the cinnamon, paprika, mint and half of the pepper. Place chicken on broiler pan or foil-lined baking sheet; brush 1 side with half of the spice mixture.

2 Broil chicken, turning halfway through and brushing with remaining spice mixture, for about 15 minutes or until glazed and no longer pink inside. Meanwhile, in saucepan, heat remaining oil over medium heat; cook garlic, onion and remaining salt and pepper, stirring occasionally, for 5 minutes or until softened.

3 Add 1 cup (250 mL) water, remaining orange juice and apricots; bring to boil. Stir in couscous and zucchini; cover and remove from heat. Let stand for 5 minutes; fluff with fork. Serve with chicken. Makes 4 servings.

Cajun Rainbow Trout ◀

1-1/2 tsp	paprika	7 mL
3/4 tsp	pepper	4 mL
1/2 tsp	each salt, dried oregano, chili powder and dry mustard	2 mL
1/4 tsp	dried thyme	1 mL
Pinch	cayenne pepper	Pinch
1 lb	rainbow trout fillets (1/2 inch/1 cm thick)	500 g
2 tsp	vegetable oil	10 mL
2 tsp	chopped fresh parsley	10 mL
1	green onion, chopped	1
	Lemon wedges	

1 In small bowl, combine paprika, pepper, salt, oregano, chili powder, mustard, thyme and cayenne pepper; set aside.

2 Pat fillets dry; place on broiler pan, skin side down. Brush both sides of fillets with oil. Sprinkle both sides evenly with paprika mixture.

3 Broil 4 to 6 inches (10 to 15 cm) from heat for 4 to 5 minutes or until fish is opaque and flakes easily when tested with fork. Place on serving plate; sprinkle with parsley and green onion. Squeeze 1 of the lemon wedges over fish; serve with remaining wedges. Makes 4 servings.

Fish simplifies your life. It's available both fresh and good-quality frozen these days, and it takes so little time to cook it's worthwhile including it often on menus. A lovely mild blend of Cajun flavors enhances the trout without overwhelming it. Adjust the amount of cayenne if you're a spicy-hot household. The other parts of the dinner add to the beauty of the trout — crunchy green beans and rice flecked with sweet red pepper.

Per serving: about
- 160 calories
- 24 g protein
- 6 g fat
- 2 g carbohydrate
- good source of iron

TIP: To make the rice timbales, use a fork to stir the red pepper into the hot rice, press into greased custard cups, then invert onto warmed plates.

Glazed Pork Tenderloin with Chinese Noodles ▶

Entertaining may seem daunting when there's barely time after a full day's work to pick up the groceries. But with reliably tender and versatile pork tenderloin as the centerpiece of your menu, you'll have no trouble offering a stylish meal that's family — and company — friendly. The glossy hoisin sauce gives the tenderloin a luxurious glaze and dresses the stir-fried sweet pepper and noodle toss. Serve with a favorite steamed green, napa cabbage, bok choy or spinach and garnish with green onion curls.

Per serving: about
- 635 calories
- 11 g fat
- very high source of fiber
- 42 g protein
- 90 g carbohydrate
- good source of iron

TIP: Look for hoisin sauce in most supermarkets and Asian grocery stores. Once opened, store jar in refrigerator for up to several months.

2	pork tenderloins (12 oz/375 g each)	2
1 tbsp	vegetable oil	15 mL
1/2 cup	hoisin sauce	125 mL
2 tbsp	minced gingerroot	25 mL
2 tbsp	each soy sauce and red wine vinegar	25 mL
1 tbsp	liquid honey	15 mL
2	cloves garlic, minced	2
1-1/2 tsp	toasted sesame seeds	7 mL
2	pkg (400 g each) precooked Chinese noodles	2
1	onion, thinly sliced	1
1	each sweet green and red pepper, thinly sliced	1
1 tbsp	lemon juice	15 mL

1 Fold narrow ends of pork under. In skillet, heat oil over high heat; sear pork all over, about 5 minutes. Place on broiler pan or on rack on foil-lined baking sheet. Whisk together hoisin sauce, ginger, soy sauce, vinegar, honey and garlic; set 1/2 cup (125 mL) aside. Brush half of the remaining sauce over pork.

2 Broil 6 inches (15 cm) from heat, turning halfway through and brushing with remaining sauce, for 10 to 12 minutes or until juices run clear when pork is pierced and just a hint of pink remains inside. Sprinkle with sesame seeds; tent with foil. Let stand for 5 minutes; thinly slice on the diagonal.

3 Loosen noodles under cold water. In bowl, cover noodles with boiling water; let stand for 4 minutes. Drain. Meanwhile, in skillet, cook onion and green and red peppers over medium-high heat for 5 minutes. Add lemon juice and reserved sauce; cook for 1 minute. Toss with noodles; serve with pork. Makes 6 servings.

Sirloin Sizzle ◄

1-1/2 lb	top sirloin steak, 3/4 inch (2 cm) thick	750 g
3 tbsp	cider vinegar	50 mL
2 tbsp	ketchup	25 mL
1 tbsp	each fancy molasses and Worcestershire sauce	15 mL
1	clove garlic, minced	1
1 tsp	dried oregano	5 mL
1/2 tsp	ground cumin	2 mL
1/4 tsp	pepper	1 mL
Pinch	salt	Pinch

1 Place steak in large shallow dish. Whisk together vinegar, ketchup, molasses, Worcestershire sauce, garlic, oregano, cumin, pepper and salt; pour over steak, turning to coat. Let stand for 10 minutes.

2 Reserving marinade, place steak on greased grill over medium-high heat; close lid and cook, turning and basting with marinade once, for about 10 minutes or until browned and springy to the touch for rare, or to desired doneness.

3 To test for doneness, use tip of pointed sharp knife to make small slit in steak. Transfer to cutting board; tent with foil and let stand for about 5 minutes before slicing across the grain. Makes 6 servings.

TIPS

● If you want to prepare the steak ahead of time, add 2 tbsp (25 mL) of vegetable oil to the marinade. Cover and marinate in refrigerator for up to 8 hours.

● Turn steak with tongs, never a fork, to avoid piercing meat and letting the juices run out.

Make any day a fiesta with a succulent steak. In choosing a sirloin or other larger piece of beef, there's less fussing with turning numerous individual steaks on the barbecue. But the real advantage to a thick sirloin is that it slices beautifully and, arranged on a warm platter, lets everyone tailor the serving size to suit.

Per serving: about
- 143 calories
- 21 g protein
- 5 g fat
- 3 g carbohydrate
- good source of iron

Pork Chops with Corn Salsa ▲

Because pork chops are now so lean, you have to watch them carefully on the grill so they don't overcook and toughen. Take them off when the juices run clear.

Per serving: about
• 213 calories   • 21 g protein
• 9 g fat   • 13 g carbohydrate

1 tbsp	vegetable oil	15 mL
1 tsp	chili powder	5 mL
Pinch	salt	Pinch
4	boneless pork chops	4
1-1/2 cups	salsa	375 mL
3/4 cup	corn kernels	175 mL
1	tomato, chopped	1
1 tbsp	chopped fresh coriander or parsley	15 mL

● Combine oil, chili powder and salt; brush over both sides of chops. Place on greased grill over medium heat; close lid and cook, turning once, for about 10 minutes or until juices run clear when pork is pierced and just a hint of pink remains inside.

● Meanwhile, combine salsa, corn, tomato and coriander; serve over chops. Makes 4 servings.

TIP: Bone-in pork chops work equally well in this recipe. However, though boneless are more expensive, they tend to be better value because you don't pay for bone and excess fat.

Barbecue Steamed Mussels

2 lb	mussels	1 kg
1-1/2 cups	chopped drained canned tomatoes	375 mL
1/2 cup	white wine or chicken stock	125 mL
2	green onions, chopped	2
2	cloves garlic, minced	2
1 tbsp	chopped fresh oregano (or 1/2 tsp/2 mL dried)	15 mL
1/4 tsp	crushed fennel seeds (optional)	1 mL
Dash	hot pepper sauce	Dash

● Scrub mussels, removing beards; discard any that do not close when tapped. In 8-inch (2 L) foil pan, combine tomatoes, wine, green onions, garlic, oregano, fennel seeds (if using) and hot pepper sauce. Nestle mussels into sauce, spooning sauce over top. Tent with foil, pinching tightly to edge.

● Place on grill over medium-high heat; close lid and cook, shaking container twice to baste, for about 15 minutes or until mussels open. Discard any that do not open. Makes 2 servings.

The mussels steam to succulence as they pick up the tomato and herb flavors of the sauce. Grill a halved baguette alongside to tear off chunks and sop up the sauce. A sprinkling of chopped fresh parsley or green onions makes an easy garnish.

Per serving: about
- 176 calories
- 3 g fat
- excellent source of iron
- 18 g protein
- 15 g carbohydrate

Lemon Rosemary Chicken for Two

2	chicken legs	2
2	cloves garlic	2
2 tsp	grated lemon rind	10 mL
2 tbsp	lemon juice	25 mL
1 tbsp	chopped fresh rosemary (or 1 tsp/5 mL dried)	15 mL
2 tsp	granulated sugar	10 mL
1/2 tsp	soy sauce	2 mL
1/4 tsp	each salt and pepper	1 mL
1 tsp	cornstarch	5 mL

● Place chicken in microwaveable dish just large enough to arrange in single layer. With flat side of large knife, crush garlic. Combine garlic, lemon rind and juice, rosemary, sugar, soy sauce, salt and pepper; pour over chicken, turning to coat. Cover and microwave at High, turning chicken and basting once, for about 7 minutes or until juices run still slightly pink when legs are pierced.

● Reserving marinade, place chicken on greased grill over medium-high heat; close lid and cook, turning once, for 10 minutes or until juices run clear when chicken is pierced.

● Meanwhile, whisk cornstarch into 1/4 cup (50 mL) cold water; whisk into juices in dish. Microwave at High for 1 minute or until slightly thickened, whisking halfway through. Discard garlic. Serve as dipping sauce with chicken. Makes 2 servings.

Using the microwave oven in tandem with the barbecue puts wonderful smoky flavors on the table in no time. Serve with new potatoes and green beans.

Per serving: about
- 305 calories
- 17 g fat
- 30 g protein
- 8 g carbohydrate

Provençale Pizza Pie ▶

To make homemade crust for pizza in under 30 minutes is a tall order. However, with a biscuit base it's almost possible and, with a few minutes' grace, you can do it using frozen broccoli, tuna and olives. Substitute other favorite toppings, if desired. While the pizza bakes, toss a tomato and lettuce salad to serve alongside.

Per serving: about
- 450 calories   • 25 g protein
- 20 g fat   • 43 g carbohydrate
- excellent source of calcium and iron

TIP: Plan ahead by mixing all the dry ingredients beforehand, so it's just a matter of adding oil and buttermilk — and you have the pizza base.

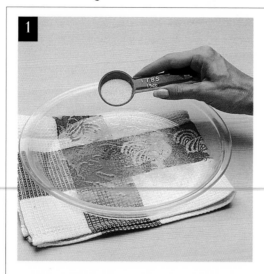

1/3 cup	cornmeal	75 mL
1/2 cup	whole wheat flour	125 mL
1/2 cup	all-purpose flour	125 mL
1/2 tsp	each baking powder, baking soda and dried basil	2 mL
1/4 tsp	salt	1 mL
1/2 cup	buttermilk	125 mL
2 tbsp	olive oil	25 mL
	FILLING	
1-1/2 cups	frozen broccoli florets, thawed	375 mL
3	green onions, chopped	3
10	olives, pitted and quartered	10
1	can (3 oz/85 g) water-packed tuna, drained and broken in chunks	1
5	marinated artichokes, halved	5
1/2 tsp	dried thyme	2 mL
1/4 tsp	pepper	1 mL
1-1/2 cups	shredded part-skim mozzarella cheese	375 mL

1 Sprinkle 1 tbsp (15 mL) of the cornmeal over side and bottom of greased 9-inch (23 cm) glass pie plate; set aside.

2 In bowl, combine whole wheat and all-purpose flours, remaining cornmeal, baking powder, baking soda, basil and salt; mix in buttermilk and oil. Turn out onto work surface; knead about 10 times to form smooth dough. Press evenly over bottom and 1 inch (2.5 cm) up side of pie plate.

3 FILLING: Top crust with broccoli, onions, olives, tuna, artichokes, thyme and pepper; sprinkle with mozzarella cheese. Bake in 375°F (190°C) oven for about 25 minutes or until crust is golden on bottom. If desired, broil for 2 to 3 minutes until cheese is golden. Makes 4 servings.

Balsamic Chicken and Roasted Vegetables ◀

4	plum tomatoes	4
12	mushrooms	12
3 tbsp	freshly grated Parmesan cheese	50 mL
4	chicken breasts (1 lb/500 g)	4
	Salt and pepper	.
	SAUCE	
1/3 cup	balsamic vinegar	75 mL
1/3 cup	tomato juice	75 mL
3 tbsp	olive oil	50 mL
2 tbsp	chopped fresh thyme (or 2 tsp/10 mL dried)	25 mL
2 tbsp	Dijon mustard	25 mL
1 tbsp	granulated sugar	15 mL
2	cloves garlic, minced	2

1 SAUCE: In small saucepan, whisk together vinegar, tomato juice, oil, thyme, mustard, sugar and garlic; bring to boil over high heat. Boil, whisking occasionally, for 5 minutes or until thick enough to coat back of spoon. Set aside 1/4 cup (50 mL) to serve with chicken.

2 Halve tomatoes lengthwise. Remove mushroom stems. Arrange vegetables, cut side up, in 13- x 9-inch (3.5 L) cake pan. Spoon half of the sauce over mushrooms only; sprinkle both vegetables with Parmesan cheese. Bake on lower rack of 400°F (200°C) oven for 10 minutes.

3 Pull skin from chicken; score 3 times. Place on broiler pan; coat with some of the remaining sauce. Broil, turning and brushing with sauce once, for 12 to 15 minutes or until no longer pink inside. Season chicken and vegetables with salt and pepper to taste. Serve with reserved sauce. Makes 4 servings.

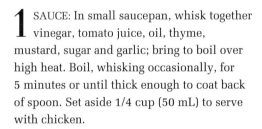

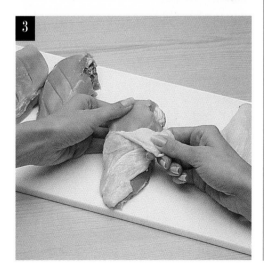

Author and food writer Dana McCauley created this quick take on a roasted chicken dinner. While the chicken broils on the top rack of the oven, tomatoes and mushrooms drizzled with a tangy sauce roast to perfection underneath. Serve with spinach linguine or other colorful pasta.

Per serving: about
- 290 calories
- 31 g protein
- 14 g fat
- 11 g carbohydrate
- good source of iron

TIP: Plum tomatoes hold their shape best.

The Contributors

For your easy reference, we have included an alphabetical listing of recipes by contributor.

Elizabeth Baird
Asparagus Salmon Salad, 23
Salsa Ranchero, 62
Tomato Beef Stir-Fry, 50

Vicki Burns
Beef Kibbe Patties, 66
Minestrone in Minutes, 33

Pam Collacott
Instant Egg Fajita, 74

Janet Cornish
Deli Rice Salad Supper, 18

Cynthia David
Chick-Pea Quesadillas, 62
Saucy Sausage Supper, 6
Veggie Quesadillas, 62

Carol Ferguson
Greek Pasta Salad, 21
Potato Salad with
    Shrimp, 20

**Shannon Ferrier
and Tamara Shuttleworth**
Curried Vegetables, 59

Margaret Fraser
Fusilli with Ham and
    Peas, 15
Garden Vegetable Stir-Fry
    for One, 53

Kate Gammal
Pork Chop Skillet
    Supper, 39

Heather Howe
Asian Beef and Noodle
    Stir-Fry, 49
Grilled Chicken Pasta
    Salad, 26
White Bean Soup with
    Carrot Salsa, 29

Anne Lindsay
Barbecued Quesadillas, 63
Ginger Chicken, 52
Picadillo, 58
Thai Chicken Curry, 46

Jan Main
Stir-Fry Pork Tenderloin
    Salad, 25

Dana McCauley
Balsamic Chicken and
    Roasted Vegetables, 89

Rose Murray
Chinese-Style Quickie
    Noodle Soup, 34
Sautéed Hoisin Orange
    Chicken, 36

Daphna Rabinovitch
Chicken Fried Rice, 42
Exotic Sloppy Joes, 72
Green Bean and Chicken
    Caesar Salad, 24
Mango Curried Chicken, 55
Update on Swedish
    Meatballs, 45

Iris Raven
Turkey Hot Pot — Olé, 30

Bonnie Stern
Lemony Breaded Pork, 41
Pasta with Tomato Sauce
    and Greens, 10
Stir-Fry Tofu and
    Vegetables, 52

**Canadian Living Test
Kitchen**
Antipasto Toss for Two, 16
Barbecue Steamed
    Mussels, 85
Bean Burgers with
    Coriander Cream, 67
Bulgur Tuna Tabbouleh, 20
Cajun Rainbow Trout, 79
Cajun Rice and Beans, 59
Cheesy Tortellini, 12
Chicken Burritos, 75
Chicken Roll-Ups, 71
Clean-Out-the-Crisper
    Creamy Soup, 30
Couscous and Chick-Pea
    Burgers, 69
Creamy Mushroom and
    Chicken Toss, 17
Creamy Tomato Shells, 11
Fresh Coleslaw Reubens, 63
Glazed Pork Tenderloin
    with Chinese Noodles, 60
Grilled Sausage
    Sandwiches, 65
Heartwarming Hamburger
    Soup, 31
Herbed Pork Cutlets, 41
Hurry Curried Lamb, 56
Kid-Pleasing Chicken
    Soup, 34
Lemon Rosemary Chicken
    for Two, 85

Photography Credits

LAURA ARSIE: cover photograph of Elizabeth Baird; photograph of the Canadian Living Test Kitchen staff.

FRED BIRD: pages 13, 57, 61, 64, 78, 87.

DOUGLAS BRADSHAW: pages 32, 48, 70, 81.

CHRISTOPHER CAMPBELL: all step-by-step photography; pages 54, 73.

PETER CHOU: pages 7, 75.

YVONNE DUIVENVOORDEN: pages 10, 17.

MICHAEL MAHOVLICH: page 19.

VINCENT NOGUCHI: pages 4, 25, 35, 47.

MICHAEL VISSER: page 58.

MICHAEL WARING: pages 28, 67.

ROBERT WIGINGTON: front cover; pages 14, 23, 27, 31, 37, 38, 43, 44, 51, 77, 82, 84, 88.

In the Canadian Living Test Kitchen. Clockwise from left: Elizabeth Baird (food director), Heather Howe (manager), Susan Van Hezewijk, Emily Richards, Donna Bartolini (associate food director), Daphna Rabinovitch (associate food director) and Jennifer MacKenzie.

Special Thanks

I always enjoy the moment when it comes time to acknowledge all the people who have contributed to a *Canadian Living's Best* title, starting off with the staff at *Canadian Living.* Thanks go to associate food directors Daphna Rabinovitch and Donna Bartolini, test kitchen manager Heather Howe and assistants Jennifer MacKenzie, Susan Van Hezewijk and Emily Richards. Managing editor Susan Antonacci, senior editor Julia Armstrong, editorial assistant Olga Goncalves plus the art department under Cate Cochran and copy department under Michael Killingsworth personify the excellence in initial preparation for the food pages of *Canadian Living* — excellence that translates into these beautiful cookbooks with tested-till-perfect recipes. Senior Editor Beverley Renahan is part of this team and also contributes to the meticulous copy editing of the recipes for book publication. I appreciate the support from our leaders, editor-in-chief Bonnie Cowan and publisher Caren King, in taking *Canadian Living* food beyond the pages of the magazine.

Our food writers (listed on p. 90) are especially valued contributors to the magazine and the cookbooks. Their imaginative, workable recipes are key to the success of all our cookbooks. Rightly valued are our photographers, noted above. Joining forces with the creative photographers are equally creative food stylists: they include Ruth Gangbar, Debbi Charendoff Moses, Rosemarie Superville, Lucie Richard, Olga Truchan, Jennifer McLagan, Sharon Dale and Kathy Robertson. Well-chosen props and backgrounds are equally essential. All this is organized by prop stylists who include Maggi Jones, Janet Walkinshaw, Shelly Tauber, Bridget Sargeant and Susan Doherty-Hannaford. Nutritional analysis for all our recipes comes from Info Access in the persons of Sharyn Joliat and Barbara Selley.

A warm round of applause to Wanda Nowakowska, associate editorial director at Madison Press Books, a great lover of good-looking and good-tasting books. Help from Tina Gaudino and others at Madison Press is very much appreciated. At Random House, members of the marketing and publicity departments — Kathy Bain, Pat Cairns, Sheila Kay and Cathy Paine — deserve sincere thanks, as does Duncan Shields, mass marketing sales manager (Ballantine Books). They will not rest until everyone in Canada knows what great value each and every one of the *Best* cookbooks is. Contributing support to the series are Random House president and publisher David Kent and Madison Press Books president Albert Cummings.

Elizabeth Baird

Index

Trust Canadian Living to bring you the BEST!

Watch for more new books in the months ahead.